GLOBETROTTER

TRAVEL GUIDE

MALAYSIA

HELEN OON

NEW
HOLLAND

GLOBETROTTER

TRAVEL GUIDE

First published in 1995 by
New Holland (Publishers) Ltd
London • Cape Town • Sydney

ISBN 1 85368 358 2

New Holland (Publishers) Ltd
24 Nutford Place, London W1H 6DQ

Commissioning Editor: Tim Jollands
Editor: Beverley Jollands
Design: Philip Mann, ACE Ltd
Cartography: Globetrotter Travel Maps/ML
Design, London

Typeset by Philip Mann, ACE Ltd
Reproduction by Dot Gradations Ltd, South
Woodham Ferrers
Printed and bound in Singapore by Tien Wah
Press (Pte) Ltd

All photographs by **Gerald Cubitt** with the
exception of the following:
Malaysia Tourism Promotion Board: pages 26,
27, 39, 55, 80; **Radin Mohammed Noh**: cover
(top right), pages 10, 12, 15, 17, 20, 21, 22, 23, 29,
30, 35 (top), 37, 50, 56, 57, 63, 64, 66, 79, 86, 87, 90,
91 (bottom), 93.

The publishers, author and photographer
gratefully acknowledge the generous assistance
during the compilation of this book of:

The Malaysia Tourism Promotion Board
(London and Kuala Lumpur)
Malaysia Airlines, Kuala Lumpur
Hotel Istana, Kuala Lumpur
Concorde Hotel, Kuala Lumpur
Mutiara Beach Resort, Penang
Pelangi Beach Resort, Langkawi
Strawberry Park Resort, Cameron Highlands
Pangkor Laut Resort
Kuching Hilton, Kuching
Sabah Tourism Promotion Corporation
Borneo Adventure, Kuching

Front cover photographs
Top left: *Iban women, displaying traditional silver
jewellery, at a longhouse in Sarawak*. **Top right**:
Bangau boats on a beach near Kota Bharu. **Bottom
right**: *Silvered leaf monkey mother and baby in a
forest in Peninsular Malaysia*. **Bottom left**: *The
Masjid Jamek, one of Kuala Lumpur's most beautiful
buildings*.

Title page photograph
*The Segama River, winding through the rainforest in
Sabah*.

CONTENTS

1
Introducing Malaysia

The boundless beauty of the enchanting land of Malaysia has captivated many a traveller's heart. For centuries, traders and explorers were drawn to its shores to seek their fortune or to find a congenial place to settle down. From the four corners of the world came languages and customs which blended with the rich traditions of the indigenous population to create a diverse and fascinating culture.

Blessed with perpetual sunshine, this is an all-year-round holiday destination. For adventure seekers, the lofty summit of **Mount Kinabalu** beckons invitingly and the awesome **Mulu Caves** are waiting to be explored. A visit to a **Sarawak longhouse** is unforgettable, and a trek into the primeval rainforest of **Taman Negara** is not to be missed. The miles of golden sand along the **East Coast** of Peninsular Malaysia are a haven for sun-worshippers and watersport enthusiasts. The gourmet will be spoilt for choice, whether at a humble hawker's stall or dining in smart hotels. For shoppers, **Kuala Lumpur** and **Penang** offer a seemingly endless selection of bargains.

Malaysia boasts well-developed rail (in Peninsular Malaysia) and road systems that make the whole country easily accessible from gateway cities which are also well served by air. Political stability and a booming economy make it a safe and attractive place as a holiday or business destination. Tourism has fortunately not changed the character of the people: on the contrary it has encouraged them to preserve and share their rich heritage. The friendliness of its people makes Malaysia irresistible.

TOP ATTRACTIONS

*** **Kuala Lumpur**: a city of vivid architectural contrasts.
*** **Taman Negara**: a vast unspoilt tract of the world's oldest and most diverse tropical rainforest.
*** **The East Coast**: the best beaches in Malaysia and traditional village life.
*** **The island of Penang**: the Pearl of the Orient.
*** **Mount Kinabalu**: Southeast Asia's highest mountain, a botanical treasure trove.
*** **Sarawak**: a wild and beautiful setting for riverborne adventure.

Opposite: *Tropical paradise: golden sand, calm blue sea and shady palms on Pulau Tioman, a tiny island off the East Coast.*

THE LAND

Peninsular (or West) Malaysia straddles the equator, stretching from Thailand in the north to Singapore in the south. To the east, 600km (370 miles) across the South China Sea, is East Malaysia, comprising the states of Sarawak and Sabah in the northern part of **Borneo**. Together they constitute the country of Malaysia which consists of 13 states – Johor, Negeri Sembilan, Melaka, Pahang, Terengganu, Kelantan, Perak, Pérlis, Kedah, Selangor, Penang, Sarawak, Sabah and the Federal Territory of Kuala Lumpur and Labuan (Borneo).

The mountains of the **Banjaran Titiwangsa**, or Main Range, which sprawl from the Thai border to Negeri Sembilan, form the main backbone of the Malaysian Peninsula, blockading the western region from the east.

Given the configuration of its physical features and the heavy rainfall, Malaysia is criss-crossed with rivers which still form the main arteries for transport, particularly in the rural areas. On the west coast of Peninsular Malaysia, Sarawak and Sabah, alluvial coastal plains, usually fringed with mangrove swamps, are backed by the rugged mountainous interior. The east coast of the Peninsula has long stretches of fine sandy beach running from **Kelantan** in the north to **Johor** in the southern tip of the country.

Climate

The proximity of Malaysia to the equator gives it a decidedly **tropical climate**. Temperatures are high all year round, averaging 26°C (80°F) in the coastal lowlands. The hill resorts enjoy a slightly cooler climate – **Cameron Highlands** in Pahang, for instance, has a mean temperature of 18°C (65°F). Humidity is high, averaging 80%. The **northeast monsoon** blows across the South China Sea from October to March, bringing heavy rain to the east coasts

WHAT TO WEAR

In view of the hot humid weather, it is advisable to wear light clothing of cotton or silk. Informality is the order of the day, with smart casual clothes for evenings if you are dining out at a restaurant. For formal functions, men normally wear suits and ties or the Malaysian costume of long-sleeved batik shirts. For jungle trekking, it is advisable to wear light cotton long pants tucked tightly into your socks and trainers to avoid being bitten by leeches and mosquitoes. (Always carry some water and insect repellent when travelling in the interior or rural areas.)

of Malaysia, Sarawak and Sabah. Kedah and Perlis, however, lying too far north to be affected by the northeast monsoon, go through a dry spell during this period. The **southwest monsoon** between May and September conveys drier weather to the whole country with the exception of the west coast, which experiences some rain in this season. Even in the wettest months it seldom rains all day long, but it can cause inconvenience during trips to the interior for forest trekking or longhouse river safaris.

Above: *Tropical rainforest in Taman Negara, Pahang.*
Opposite: *The view from Low's Peak at the summit of Mount Kinabalu in Sabah.*

Plant Life

About four-fifths of the land mass of Malaysia is covered with **tropical rainforest**. The vegetation varies according to the elevation of the land. The forest consists of freshwater **swamps** of mangrove and Nipa palms in the alluvial coastal regions, **dipterocarps** in the lowland forest and **heath** and **montane forests** in the hilly and rocky areas especially in Sarawak and Sabah. Wild **orchids** and bright flowers occur but they are frequently hidden in the thick green foliage of the lush forests or perched high up on the tall green canopy of the trees. The tropical Malaysian forests contain an amazing

RAINFOREST TREES

The largest trees in the lowland rainforest may grow as high as 45m (147ft) or more and up to 3m (10ft) in circumference. These forest giants are all members of a single plant family, the dipterocarps, so named because their seeds usually have two wings (di = two; ptero = wing; carp = seed). In spite of their size, they grow slowly, and some are many hundreds of years old.

number of plant species with an estimated 8,000 species of flowering plants of which 2,500 are trees. It is quite common to find a hundred species of trees on a single hectare. Land that has previously been cleared for agriculture grows coarse tall elephant grass or *lallang*, while in the urban areas rain-trees and flamboyant trees of fiery coloured flowers are commonly found.

The Animal Kingdom

The wealth and variety of vegetation in the rainforest sustains an amazing proliferation of wildlife. The natural orchestra of the forest is normally led by the shrieks of the various species of monkeys swinging in the tree-tops, the maniacal laughter of the hornbills, the sporadic melodious songs of the *merbuk* (doves) or magpie-robin and the grunting of wild boars, rising above the incessant chorus of the cicadas and crickets. Snakes or big game animals are seldom seen in the Malaysian forest. Unlike the African safaris where tourists can see wild animals in full view from the comfort of a jeep, here one would need to exercise great patience to view a tiger or a leopard. In **Taman Negara** National Park in Pahang visitors can perch high up in wildlife hides to spy on the animals, but the thick foliage of the forest provides

excellent hiding-places and camouflage for its inhabitants.

Amongst the carnivores, the tiger is the pride of Malaysia and adorns the armorial ensigns of the nation. Clouded leopards and other wild cats are occasionally encountered while the *musang* (civet cat) is more commonly seen at the edge of villages or plantations. The sun bear is the largest of the

Left: *A dusky leaf monkey (also known as the spectacled langur) in the forest on Penang Hill.*
Opposite: *The magnificent Rajah Brooke's birdwing, a species of butterfly discovered by the naturalist Alfred Russel Wallace. It has a wingspan of up to 17cm (7in).*

omnivores in Malaysia and can be hunted only under licence. Asian elephants, smaller than their African cousins, are quite prolific in number. They move in medium-sized herds and are known to cause havoc and destruction in fruit plantations. Less commonly found is the largest member of the wild ox family in the world, the *seladang*, which can weigh anything up to 1500kg (1.5 tons). The Sumatran rhinoceros and the tapir (which resembles a wild pig with a soft trunk-like nose) are protected species. Other smaller animals found here are deer, bats, pigs and a wide variety of monkeys, including the pig-tailed macaques which are trained to harvest coconuts in the east coast region. Orang-utans and the long-nosed proboscis monkeys (known as *orang belanda*, which means 'Dutchman') are found only in the wilds of **Sarawak** and **Sabah**. Amphibians and reptiles are plentiful and include crocodiles, monitor lizards, frogs and marine turtles, of which the most famous is the giant leatherback turtle found along the shores of **Rantau Abang** in Terengganu. Malaysia boasts 111 species of snakes and a wide variety of insects and other tropical invertebrates.

MALAYSIA'S LITTLE HERO

Pelandok and *kancil* are the local names for the lesser mouse-deer, a tiny animal about 20cm (8in) high, and not a true deer at all. In Malay folklore, however, this little creature stands tall, for he is the hero of many stories, outwitting much larger animals with his cunning and bravery. According to legend, Prince Parameswara founded the city of Melaka on the site where he had watched a mouse-deer fight off one of his own hunting dogs and drive it into the sea. Much hunted for its delicate flesh, the lesser mouse-deer is now a protected species.

HISTORY IN BRIEF

Situated in the heart of Southeast Asia at one of the world's major crossroads, Malaysia has always been pivotal to trade routes from Europe, the Orient, India and China. Its warm tropical climate and abundant natural blessings made it a congenial destination for immigrants as early as 5,000 years ago when the ancestors of the **Orang Asli**, the indigenous peoples of Peninsular Malaysia, settled here, probably the pioneers of a general movement from China and Tibet. They were followed by the **Malays**, who brought with them skills in farming and the use of metals. Around the first century BC, strong trading links were established with **China** and **India**, and these had a major impact on the culture, language and social customs of the country. Evidence of a Hindu-Buddhist period in the history of Malaysia can today be found in the temple sites of the Bujang Valley and Merbok Estuary in Kedah in the north west of Peninsular Malaysia, near the Thai border. The spread of **Islam**, introduced by Arab and Indian traders, brought the Hindu-Buddhist era to an end by the 13th century. With the conversion of the Malay-Hindu rulers of the **Melaka Sultanate** (the Malay kingdom which ruled both

HISTORICAL CALENDAR

c1400 Founding of Melaka by Prince Parameswara.
1511 Melaka conquered by Portuguese. Malay Sultanate re-established in Johor.
1541 Portuguese rule in Melaka overthrown by Dutch.
1699 Sultan Mahmud murdered, ending Melakan dynasty.
1786 Francis Light founds British trading settlement on Penang.
1819 Thomas Stamford Raffles establishes trading post on Singapore.
1824 Anglo-Dutch Treaty of London confirms Dutch rule in Indonesian archipelago; Britain retains Straits Settlements (Penang, Melaka and Singapore).
1841 James Brooke becomes

first 'White Rajah' of Sarawak.
1874 Treaty of Pangkor establishes British Residential system, introducing British administration throughout Peninsular Malaysia.
1881 Establishment of British North Borneo Company in present-day Sabah.
1895–1900 Mat Salleh's rebellion in British North Borneo.
1896 Formation of Federated Malay States (Perak, Pahang, Negeri Sembilan and Selangor) as British Protectorate, with Kuala Lumpur as its capital.
1909 Acceptance of British Residents by Kedah, Perlis, Kelantan and Terengganu (Unfederated Malay States).
1914 Johor becomes last state to enter Malay Federation.

1941–45 Japanese occupation.
1948 Creation of Federation of Malaya and beginning of Malayan Emergency.
1957 Malaya declared independent.
1963 Malaya joined by Sarawak, Sabah and Singapore to create Malaysia, under first PM Tunku Abdul Rahman.
1963–6 Indonesian *Konfrontasi* campaign.
1965 Singapore becomes republic.
1969 Racial tension culminates in May 13 Riots and emergency rule.
1971 Formation of new national ideology designed to overcome ethnic differences.
1981 Dato' Seri Dr Mahathir bin Mohamad becomes Malaysia's fourth PM.

sides of the Straits of Melaka for over a hundred years), Islam was established as the religion of the Malays, and had a profound effect on Malay society.

The arrival of Europeans in Malaysia brought a dramatic change to the country. In 1511, the **Portuguese** captured Melaka and the rulers of the Melaka Sultanate fled south to Johor where they tried to establish a new kingdom. They were resisted not only by the Europeans but by the Acehnese, Minangkabau and the Bugis, resulting in the sovereign units of the present-day states of Peninsular Malaysia. The Portuguese were in turn defeated in 1641 by the **Dutch**, who colonized Melaka until the advent of the **British** in the late 18th century. Neither the Portuguese nor the Dutch exerted any profound influence on Malay society. The British acquired Melaka from the Dutch in 1824 in exchange for Bencoolen in Sumatra. From their new bases in Melaka, Penang and Singapore, collectively known as the Straits Settlements, the British, through their influence and power, began the process of political integration of the Malay states of Peninsular Malaysia.

Opposite: *Georgetown, Penang in 1814. As a free port Penang was enjoying unrivalled commercial success at this time.*

Melaka's town square in 1845, showing the Dutch Stadthuys and Christ Church.

MAT SALLEH

The British North Borneo Company obtained a royal charter in 1881, but was never a commercial success. Though its founders hoped to make their fortunes first from gold and later tobacco, they were disappointed and had to rely largely on the collection of taxes. A tax on rice – the staple food – was amongst the grievances that led Mat Salleh to rebel against the British in 1895. The son of a Sulu chief, Mat Salleh aquired legendary status in his lifetime: it was said that he could throw a buffalo by its horns, that flames leapt from his mouth when he spoke and that his knife flashed lightning. His rebellion was well organized and based on a series of strongly defended forts. After he was shot during the siege of his fort at Tambunan in 1900 his followers continued their attacks on the British for a further five years.

Meanwhile, in Borneo, the states of Sarawak and Sabah, although under the nominal rule of the ancient kingdom of Brunei, had lived an autonomous existence until the 19th century. In 1840, a British adventurer, James Brooke, who had helped to quell local rebellions and fought against piracy in Sarawak, was made Rajah by the Sultan of Brunei as a reward.

With the signing of the Pangkor Treaty in 1874, the British imposed direct supervision on the states of Perak and Selangor and in 1896, these, together with Negeri Sembilan and Pahang, formed the Federated Malay States with Kuala Lumpur as the capital. By 1914, the Unfederated Malay States of Johor, Kedah, Kelantan, Perlis and Terengganu had come under British rule. The East Malaysian states of Sabah and Sarawak became British protectorates in 1888.

After World War II and the Japanese occupation from 1941-45, the British created the Malayan Union in 1946. This was abandoned in 1948 and the Federation of Malaya emerged in its place. The Federation gained its independence from Britain on 31 August 1957. In September 1963, Malaya, Sarawak, Sabah, and initially Singapore united to form Malaysia, a country whose potpourri of society and customs derives from its rich heritage from four of the world's major cultures – Chinese, Indian, Islamic and Western.

GOVERNMENT AND ECONOMY

Malaysia is a constitutional monarchy with the king, known as the **Yang di-Pertuan Agong**, as its supreme head of state. The king is elected every five years by his fellow rulers of the royal states of Johor, Selangor, Perak, Pahang, Kelantan, Terengganu, Kedah, Perlis and Negeri Sembilan, who act on the advice of the state executive council. The non-royal states of Penang, Melaka, Sarawak and Sabah are headed by governors, appointed on a four-yearly basis. They act in accordance with the advice of the respective state government which is headed by a chief minister. The state government is run along the guidelines of the federal government in Kuala Lumpur, and every elected king has to act in accordance with government advice. The country has a parliamentary democratic government, elected every five years: there is universal suffrage. The head of government is the prime minister. The parliament has two houses: the Dewan Negara (the upper house), with 58 members, and the Dewan Rakyat.

Economic Development

When Malaysia gained its independence from the British in 1957, it was the world's largest producer of **tin** and **rubber**. Whilst it enjoyed prosperity from these sources,

The main gateway of the Istana Negara in Kuala Lumpur, official residence of the Yang di-Pertuan Agong, the king of Malaysia.

Tourism now plays a major part in Malaysia's economic success and the country boasts some very luxurious resorts. This inviting swimming pool belongs to the Golden Sands Hotel at Batu Feringghi, Penang's most famous beach.

TOURISM
A BOOMING INDUSTRY

The first 'Visit Malaysia Year' in 1990 reportedly boosted visitor arrivals by 56%, and following this success a second campaign was launched in 1994. With its massive potential as a holiday destination, Malaysia aims to attract 20 million visitors to the country by the year 2000.

---

it was also at the mercy of price fluctuations in the world markets. To combat this unstable situation the administration set out to diversify the economy in the agricultural sector while encouraging industrialization in selected areas. Products such as **palm oil**, **cocoa**, **pepper**, **pineapple**, **timber** and **tobacco** now play an important part in the agrarian sector. **Petroleum** and **gas** are another boon to the economy while **tourism** also makes a major contribution.

The economic strategy of the government is carried out in a series of five-year plans guided since 1971 by the **New Economic Policy** (NEP). The aim of the current plan (1991–1995) is to achieve sustained economic growth of 7.5%. In recent years, Malaysia's GDP growth rates have been among the highest in the world and the country enjoys political stability, low unemployment and a well-educated workforce in addition to an excellent infrastructure and a flourishing manufacturing sector. Malaysia encourages foreign investment with attractive incentives like tax holidays of five to ten years, the full repatriation of capital and profits, minimal exchange controls and 100% foreign equity ownership. A number of Free Trade Zones allow manufacturers in export-oriented industries to enjoy minimum customs controls and formalities. The Malaysian Industrial Development Authority (MIDA), with branches overseas, was set up to promote and co-ordinate all industrial activities. Malaysia intends to become a fully industrialized nation with a competitive and dynamic economy by the year 2020, and has formulated a new policy, **Vision 2020**, to strive towards this goal.

THE PEOPLE

Malaysian culture can best be described as a melting-pot: it is a multi-faceted society, with customs and languages as diverse as they are numerous. Settlers from China, India, and Europe have all exercised a major influence on the people and together with the strong indigenous culture, they form a society that is uniquely Malaysian. Although the lingua franca is Bahasa Malaysia (Malay), the close racial integration of the society has produced a colloquial speech derived from all the communities present. It is not unusual to hear a Malaysian using Malay, Chinese, Indian, English and even Portuguese words in one sentence. Interracial marriages are commonplace and acceptable and the children of such unions are the true Malaysians of the future.

CUSTOMS AND ETIQUETTE: DOS AND DON'TS

- Always remove shoes before entering a house or a place of worship. When visiting a mosque, women should not wear shorts or expose bare shoulders.
- It is impolite to address elderly people by their first names. Always call them 'Uncle' or 'Auntie', or 'Pah Chik' (men) and 'Mah Chik' (women) for Malays, especially in the villages.
- It is considered both bad luck and rude to refuse food and drinks, especially before you embark on a journey. Always make at least a token attempt to taste what is offered.
- Black is connected only with death and funerals, so should not be worn on joyous occasions.
- It is impolite to walk in front of people seated in a room without bowing slightly and stretching out your right hand in front of you, as a gesture denoting 'Excuse me' as you pass by.
- Never use your left hand when eating or handing something to a Malaysian as it is considered for other more 'basic' purposes only.
- It is impolite to touch anyone on the head, especially the elderly.

A fisherman mending his nets at Sungai Ular in Pahang exemplifies the gentle pace and traditional lifestyle of the East Coast of Peninsular Malaysia.

TAKING PHOTOGRAPHS

The best times for stunning shots are before 10am or after 4pm. Use slow film to counteract the bleaching effect of tropical sun, 400 asa film in the rainforest.

When taking photographs of people, remember to ask permission first. Be prepared to pay a fee if asked.

MUSIC AND DANCE

The dance and music of the Malays reflect their characteristic gentleness and grace. Many of the dances tell a story of everyday activities such as harvesting or planting rice (*tarian canggung* from Perlis and *tarian balai* from Terengganu) or fishing (*tarian cinta sayang* from Kedah). Others are court dances for the sultan (*tarian aysik* from Kelantan) or recall historical events (*tarian kuda kepang* from Johor – the story of battles fought by Muhammad and his disciples). The colourful and elaborate costumes are adorned with beautiful accessories of gold and silver and vary from state to state. A unique feature of the traditional dances is that there is no physical contact between male and female dancers as it is not customary in Malay society for an unmarried man and woman to touch each other in public.

The *bumiputra*

The *bumiputra*, or 'sons of the soil', are defined as those people whose cultures are indigenous to the region, such as the Malays, the Orang Asli of Peninsular Malaysia and the indigenous tribes of Sarawak and Sabah. Under the common bond of Islam, Malays who migrated across the Straits of Melaka from Sumatra in the late 19th and 20th century, the Javanese, especially from the western coasts of Johor, Selangor and Lower Perak, and the Bajau of Sabah who originated from the Sulu region in the Philippines are also classified as *bumiputra*. Non-Malay *bumiputra* include the indigenous tribes of Sarawak and Sabah. The *bumiputra* are granted special privileges like housing and business grants, land rights and scholarships as part of the government's policy to elevate them to equal economic status with the Chinese and certain sectors of the Indian community, who have a strong control of the economy.

The Non-*bumiputra* group

The non-*bumiputra* group consists of the Chinese, Indians and other minor communities like the Sinhalese, Eurasians and Europeans. The Chinese and Indians came to settle in Malaysia in great numbers in the 19th century due to the rapid economic development in the country brought about by the open trading policies of the British in the Straits Settlements.

The Malays

The Malays were known to have lived in Kampuchea, the Malay Peninsula and the southern seas as far back as 3000 years ago. The Malays of the Peninsula had close affinities with the Malays of Sumatra and for centuries the Straits of Melaka were not a political boundary but a passage linking the different groups of the same family. They were great navigators and had advanced farming skills, with a knowledge of metal working which enabled them to produce agricultural tools like the axe and the hoe. They invented the *kris* – a short wavy dagger which is unique to Malay culture. Their traditional beliefs were based on

animism and although they subsequently embraced Islam, their belief in the supernatural powers of nature is still very strong. The *bomoh* and *pawang* (medicine men with magical powers) are still accorded great respect.

The Malays chiefly live in the rural areas as farmers and some have smallholdings of palm oil and rubber. Those found along the coastal region are mostly fishermen or own coconut plantations. In the rural areas the life of a traditional Malay *kampung*, or village, with its wooden houses on stilts, is a communal affair. The inhabitants are self-sufficient, growing their own vegetables and fruit and keeping chickens, goats, buffaloes and cows. There is a *surau*, or small mosque, in every village, as daily life revolves around Islam. Most Malay women wear the traditional garment of *baju kurung* with sarong, while the men wear the *baju Melayu* with *sampin*, a short sarong wound round their waist. However, the *baju Melayu* is now mostly worn for official functions only as the men opt for western style clothes. With the new economic policy many Malays now play an important role in politics and commerce and the number of Malay professionals is increasing.

Malay schoolgirls at Kuala Muda in Alor Setar.

BAHASA MALAYSIA

Malay, an Austronesian language, has been augmented by various external influences, from Sanskrit in the 7th to English in the 19th century. With the advent of Islam in the 14th century, the *jawi* script was introduced and Arabic and Persian words were added to the vocabulary. Today, the language is called Bahasa Malaysia, and is now the medium of teaching from primary to university level.

In the rainforest of Taman Negara in Pahang, an Orang Asli hunter takes aim at a tree squirrel with his blowpipe.

A GIANT SWING

The Melanau celebrate the festival of the sea known as Kaul each March, when one of their traditional rituals is riding on the giant swing called a *tibow*. The wooden structure, up to 15m (50ft) high, has to be constructed without the use of nails. All joints are secured with rattan or creepers in keeping with the taboo. The occasion is one big picnic for the community and offerings and prayers are made to the sea spirits for a bountiful and safe year ahead.

The Orang Asli

Before the coming of the Malays, Peninsular Malaysia was home to the ancestors of various groups who are now collectively known as the Orang Asli, or original people. The oldest group, the **Semang**, were traditionally nomadic hunter-gatherers in the mountainous interior, constructing only temporary shelters with bamboo poles and roofs made of leaves. The **Senoi** and the **Proto-Malays** were later arrivals, many of whom practised shifting cultivation as well as fishing and hunting. Many Orang Asli now lead settled lives as farmers and are increasingly drawn into the modern economy of Malaysia, but by no means all have been lured away from their old way of life in the forest.

Indigenous peoples of East Malaysia

The **Iban** are the largest ethnic group of Sarawak and most live in longhouses along rivers in the lowland areas. Although a large number have been converted to Christianity or Islam, they still maintain a strong cultural identity and mythical heroes and deities are worshipped. Dreams and bird augury play an important part in determining their actions. The Iban are a gregarious race and enjoy merrymaking, dancing and liberal consumption of *tuak*, or rice wine, their traditional brew. Visitors to an Iban longhouse are always guaranteed a warm welcome.

The **Kayan** and **Kenyah** peoples live in the upper reaches of the Rajang and Baram Rivers in massive, carefully constructed longhouses. They are renowned for their artistic and musical skills as well as for their hospitality. In the southwest region of Sarawak live the **Bidayuh**, famous for their skills in basketry, wood and bamboo carving.

The **Melanau** live along the coast and traditionally cultivate sago as their staple crop. Most are Muslims and many have intermarried with Malays. But their former animist beliefs gave rise to the custom of carving 'sickness figures' called *belum*. After the healing ceremony, the *belum* would be left at the edge of a forest or set adrift in the river to be carried out to sea, thus taking the patient's illness with it. Melanau artisans are skilled in the building of boats and burial poles. They also display their unique craftsmanship in making decorative baskets and sunhats called *terindak*.

The **Kadazan** are the largest ethnic group of Sabah forming a third of the population of the state. They are mostly rice farmers, and many are Christians or Muslims although animism is still practised among the traditionalists. Their traditional costumes are black with gold and silver braids and diamante decorations. In the more remote regions, women still wear coiled brass necklets, anklets and bracelets. Large ceramic jars used in former times for burials now contain *tapai* or rice wine which is served freely during festivals and ceremonies.

Originally from the southern Philippines, the **Bajau** are known as the Sea Gypsies as they lead a nomadic life sailing along the coast of Semporna, Kudat and Kota Belud, coming ashore only to bury their dead.

The Chinese

The main influx of the Chinese into Malaysia was in the 19th century, some as refugees from their war-torn homeland while others came as labourers for the tin mines or to trade. Their original landing points were along the Straits of Melaka in Penang and Singapore but later they spread into other parts of the country prospecting for tin or setting up trading posts. Today the Chinese control most of the trade and industry in the country, as is evident in the bustling Chinatowns of

A Kelabit man from the old settlement at Bareo in the highlands of northern Sarawak. These hardy and self-sufficient people long ago developed sophisticated methods for growing rice and vegetables in their remote valley farms. Like other indigenous groups the Kelabit live in longhouses, but unusually these are often not partitioned: each household simply has a separate hearth around which the family sleeps.

A bustling market in one of the narrow streets of Penang's Chinatown, lined with shophouses fronted by shady 'five-foot ways'. Trishaws and motorcycles thread their way between the hawkers' stalls. Shopping here is an experience not to be missed.

LIONS AND DRAGONS

In Chinese communities, the lion dance is regularly performed at New Year and other festivals to gain compassion and good luck from the gods. Two dancers dressed as the mythical Chinese lion cavort to the beat of drums and gongs while a jester teases the beast with an ornamental ball or a cabbage. The dragon dance involves a similar ritual but more dancers are required to form the head, body and tail of the dragon which is made of bamboo and paper with an elaborately painted head. It is led by a 'warrior' with a colourful ball tied to a pole. The most impressive Chinese spectacle is the Chingay, which is practised in Penang. A team of skilled acrobats balance long poles with banners and flags on their mouths, shoulders and back and pass them from one to the other accompanied by the loud beating of drums. It is a display of great skill in balance and strength.

Kuala Lumpur (in Jalan Petaling), Penang, Alor Setar, Ipoh and most other major towns. The differing dialects and cultures of the 19th century Chinese immigrants have been preserved down the generations, as has the clan system which aided them on their arrival and contributed to their commercial success. Today the Chinese constitute about a third of Malaysia's population.

The Indians

Large numbers of Indians were brought from southern India by the British in the 19th century to work as labourers on the rubber estates and to build roads and railways. Long before this, however, a smaller number of Muslim Indians had arrived to trade in textiles. The southern Indians are Hindus and temples were established in every Indian settlement. Traditional Indian dances are still performed at festivals or weddings. Indian cuisine has a great influence on Malaysian food and culinary techniques.

RELIGION

Although Islam is the official religion of Malaysia, every section of society has the constitutional right to practise its own religion. Virtually all the world's major religions are represented here, reflecting the multi-ethnic population of the country.

Islam

Islam is recognized as the religion of the Malays although there are considerable numbers of non-Malay converts amongst the Indians, Chinese, Kadazans and other indigenous tribes in East Malaysia. Muslims form the largest single religious group in the country.

The faith was introduced to Malaysia through Indian and Arab traders but it was not until the Melaka Sultanate was converted to Islam in the 15th century that it was firmly established. It is interesting to note that in almost every hotel in Malaysia, there is always an arrow painted on the ceiling of each room pointing in the direction of Mecca. This sign, called *kiblat*, ensures that Muslim guests face towards Mecca when they observe their five-times daily prayer.

THE PILLARS OF ISLAM

The practice of Islam (which means 'submission to God') encompasses a whole way of life, and is based on five principal tenets:

Shahada: the profession of faith, that there is no god but Allah and that Muhammad is his messenger.

Salat: worship. The muezzin call the faithful to prayer five times every day, when Muslims prostrate themselves in the direction of Mecca. Friday midday prayers are especially important.

Zakat: charity. Muslims are expected to contribute a tithe each year in alms for the poor.

Saum: fasting. During the hours of daylight throughout the month of Ramadan, the faithful refrain from eating, drinking or smoking.

Haj: pilgrimage. All Muslims who can afford it undertake to make a pilgrimage to Mecca once in their lives.

A time for prayer in the Ubudiah Mosque in Kuala Kangsar, Perak. The calls of the muezzin punctuate the daily lives of all Malays.

MALAYSIA'S POPULATION

Malaysians number about
17.5 million, of whom 14.2
million live on the Peninsula,
and the remaining 3.3 million
in Sarawak and Sabah. About
half the population is Malay,
about one third Chinese, 9%
Indian and 9% indigenous
groups.

*An indian wedding in
Kuala Lumpur. The bride
and groom are enthroned
on the marriage dais, and
this practice is also
followed at Malay
weddings, a custom
retained from the Hindu
period before the coming of
Islam in the 15th century.*

Buddhism

Buddhism has the largest following in Malaysia after
Islam. It is identified primarily with the Chinese but is
also the religion of the Thais, Sinhalese and Burmese
living in the country. The establishment of the Chinese
community in Melaka in the 15th century gave
Buddhism a permanent footing, and the great waves of
immigrants from China in the late 19th century further
enhanced the spread of the religion, taking it into every
part of the country.

Hinduism

There are two phases of Hinduism in Malaysia. The early
Hindu period of the 15th century (preceding the coming
of Islam), instituted by Hindu traders, has very little to
do with the practice of Hinduism today. The aristocratic
Brahmanical Hinduism of that era was the religion of the
ruling class. Today, this form of Hinduism survives only
in some Malay language and literature, as reflected in
the traditional *wayang kulit* or shadow-puppet play and
in the Malay wedding ceremony of *bersanding* where the
bride and groom sit in state as 'king and queen for a
day'. The Hinduism practised in Malaysia today came
into the country through contract labourers who were
recruited to work in rubber and coffee plantations in the
late 19th and first half of the 20th century. Hindu
temples and institutions are diverse and the two most
popular deities worshipped are Lord Subramaniam and
Mariamman.

Sikhism

The Sikh community in Malaysia, brought into the
country as recruits for para-military units and the police
force by the British in the 1930s, settled mostly in
Penang, Perak and Selangor. The Sikh population of
Malaysia represents about 3% of the total Indian
community in the country.

Christianity

Christianity was introduced into the country by early

St George's Church in Georgetown, Penang, was the first Anglican church to be built in Southeast Asia. It was designed by Captain Robert Smith and completed in 1818. Francis Light, the founder of Georgetown, is buried in its cemetery.

traders and travellers passing through the Straits of Melaka *en route* to China. The colonization by the Portuguese in 1511, the Dutch in 1641 and later the British in 1786 set a permanent root of Christianity in the country but the faith was largely confined to the expatriate community. It was not until the 19th and 20th centuries that Christianity began to have any influence on the local people, through the work of missionaries who played a major role in the educational and medical fields by establishing schools and hospitals in various parts of the country. Their converts were notably amongst the Chinese, Indians and some indigenous tribes in East Malaysia. Today the Christian church in Malaysia is in the hands of local church leaders. The Christian population numbers about one million: 6% of the population of Malaysia.

CHRISTMAS AND EASTER

The Christians in Malaysia join the rest of the world in celebration on 25 December, with midnight mass on Christmas Eve followed by another Christmas Day service the following day. The traditions of family dinner and the exchange of gifts are observed as in western society. Departmental stores and shopping centres are ablaze with Christmas lights and festive decorations and the air is filled with carol-singing. Good Friday and Easter are observed with prayers and church services.

FESTIVALS

A significant part in Malaysia's rich cultural heritage is played by the traditional festivals of the four main groups of the population – the Malays, Chinese, Indians and the ethnic tribes of East Malaysia. They are mostly of a religious nature, but it is customary in Malaysia for the whole community to participate in all the major festivals, regardless of race or religion.

Islamic Festivals

There are three very important Islamic festivals. The Hari Raya Haji marks the conclusion of the annual pilgrimage to Mecca, when the pilgrims are given the title of Haji (for men) or Hajjah (for women). This festival falls on the tenth day of the twelfth moon in the Muslim calendar. Of a more social nature is Hari Raya Puasa, which signifies the end of the fasting season of Ramadan. The celebration is determined by the sighting of the new moon by the religious elders. This festive occasion is greeted with great joy and starts with mass prayers in the mosques. The young will ask for forgiveness from their elders and everyone will put on new clothes ready for the customary visiting of friends and relatives in an 'open-house' fashion where visitors are welcomed day and night and Malay delicacies are served to guests. Houses will have been given a thorough cleaning and decorated with coloured lights to 'welcome the angels' believed to be visiting the earth during the seven days preceding the festival. The Birthday of the Prophet Muhammad, on the twelfth day of the third moon in the Muslim calendar, is another important festival. Special prayers are offered in the mosques followed by processions.

Buddhist Festivals

The most important Buddhist festival is Vesak Day in May, which commemorates the birth, enlightenment and death of Buddha. The celebration begins at dawn when devotees congregate at the temples to pray. The sutras are chanted in unison by monks in saffron robes. Acts of charity such as feeding the needy and giving donations to the temples are carried out. The ceremony is highlighted by a candle procession by the devotees.

Chinese Festivals

New Year is the most important festival for the Chinese and is celebrated on the first day of the Chinese lunar calendar, in January or February. In the same fashion as for the Muslim celebration of Hari Raya, houses are cleaned and painted preceding the big day. Debts are settled, accounts closed and special prayers and offerings are made, particularly to the kitchen god to send him off on his annual visit to heaven. Bad language or unpleasant topics like death should not cross anyone's lips, for fear of attracting bad luck and evil spirits. Chinese characters depicting happiness, prosperity and longevity are written on red paper and pasted on front doors. Red packets, or *ang pow*, containing money in even numbers, are given to children when they visit the

Chinese dancers in traditional lion costumes perform outside the Thean Hou temple in Kuala Lumpur.

house. The festival starts with a reunion dinner for families on New Year's Eve followed by visits to one another's houses where sweetmeats and delicacies of all kinds are served. During the 'open-house' period, which is normally on the first three days of Chinese New Year, homes are open to friends from all races and religions. This is a reflection of the close racial harmony that exists amongst the people of Malaysia and the respect and acceptance of one another's religious beliefs. New Year lasts until the 15th day of the new moon, which is known as Chap Goh Mei (or Fifteenth Night).

Ching Ming, or the Festival of the Tomb, falls at the end of the second moon of the lunar year. On this day, the Chinese show their respect for their deceased ancestors by tidying up their tombs and cemeteries. Offerings of food and prayers are made in honour of their dear departed. The Moon Cake or mid-autumn festival is another colourful occasion celebrated on the 15th day of the eighth Chinese lunar calendar (in

September). This festival has historical rather than religious significance, as it marks the successful rebellion against the Mongol rulers of 14th century China. It was said that secret messages were hidden in moon cakes to spread word of the plot against the Mongolians, and lanterns were used as signals from hill-tops. Hence today, the Moon Cake Festival is celebrated with a lantern procession and moon cakes are exchanged as gifts.

Hindu Festivals

Amongst the Malaysian Indians, two major Hindu festivals are observed with great pomp and ceremony: Deepavali, or the Festivals of Lights, is celebrated in the Hindu month of Kartik in October/November. It symbolizes the mythological victory of Lord Krishna over the demon king Narakasura. It also marks a new beginning, especially for businessmen, for whom it is the start of a new financial year. On this day the Hindu celebrants wake up at the crack of dawn and bathe in herbal oil, don new clothes and say their prayers. Oil lamps are lit in every Hindu home at night to welcome Lakshmi, the goddess of wealth, who will not enter an unlit house.

Thaipusam, which falls in the Hindu month of Thai (January/February) is the celebration of the birthday of Lord Subramaniam (also known as Lord Murugan).

At the Hindu festival of Thaipusam, devotees process in a tranced state carrying spectacular decorated wooden frames, called kavadis, *supported by hooks and spikes inserted in their flesh.*

Dressed in ceremonial finery and elaborate silver jewellery, Iban dancers perform outside their longhouse.

Devotees carry *kavadis* – wooden frames decorated with peacock feathers and flowers – fastened on their bodies by metal hooks and spikes embedded in their bare flesh. Others defy all sense of pain by piercing their cheeks and tongues with metal skewers and hooks. This self-mutilation is an act of penitence in exchange for favours asked of the gods. As many as 700,000 people will turn up in Kuala Lumpur to see the procession of the celebrants in their trance-like state, dancing to the beating of drums, escorting the chariot with the statue of Lord Murugan from Maha Mariamman Temple to the temple at Batu Caves. In Penang, Thaipusam is celebrated at the Balathandaythabani Temple in Waterfall Road, while in Ipoh it is held at the Sri Subramaniam Temple at Gunung Cheroh.

Harvest Festivals of East Malaysia

Thanksgiving celebrations dedicated to the rice gods are held each May by the Kadazan of Sabah and by the Iban in Sarawak, whose festival of Gawai Dayak welcomes their New Year on 1st June. There is much merrymaking and feasting, with rice wine flowing freely throughout the festivities and traditional games, dances and beauty pageants. Everyone in the community gathers together in a true spirit of comradeship, and foreign visitors are welcome to participate in the jollity. The festivals are times for family reunions and visiting of friends with the emphasis on eating and drinking.

TRADITIONAL BELIEFS

The ancient beliefs of the indigenous peoples of Malaysia hinge on the idea of spirits that inhabit all things – mountains, rivers, trees and buildings, as well as animals and people – who need to be appeased and respected. A person's spirit resides in every part of them, and such things as their hair, sweat, shadow or their name could be used in sorcery to harm them. Children are still commonly called by nicknames rather than their real names, and older people are respectfully addressed as 'Uncle' or 'Auntie'. Many aspects of current polite behaviour have their origins in traditional beliefs and taboos.

Traditional medicine is still practised in rural areas by the *bomoh*, or magician, who uses incantations to exorcise the evil spirit causing the illness (he also invokes the name of Allah).

Offerings are made to the earth spirits to ensure good harvests, while in Sarawak the Iban sacrifice a chicken (formerly it would have been a slave) under the centre-pole of a new longhouse to appease the house spirit.

TROPICAL FRUITS

- **Durian**, 'the king of fruits': Malaysians claim it 'smells like hell and tastes like heaven': to the unfamiliar nose it just smells and tastes like hell! A giant spiky football with soft flesh with the texture of full cream cheese, wrapped around a large seed.
- **Rambutan**: skin turns red or yellow when ripe; white flesh tastes similar to a lychee.
- **Mangosteen**: segmented white juicy flesh in deep purple fleshy skin.
- **Starfruit**: soft yellow, juicy flesh has a sweet taste with a sour tang.
- **Cempedak**: greenish yellow scaly skin and golden segments of flesh containing large edible seeds.
- **Ciku**: looks similar to kiwi fruit but has a peachy flesh.

A mixed catch at the fisherman's wharf in Kota Kinabalu, Sabah. Abundant seafood is one of the glories of Malaysian cuisine.

FOOD AND DRINK

The variety of Malaysian cuisine is enough to satisfy even the most discerning epicurean. Borrowed from, and influenced by, each of its migratory populations in addition to the indigenous populace, Malaysian food and drink can aptly be described as a melting-pot of gourmet pleasure. The traditions of Chinese, Indian, Arab, Portuguese and British cooking have all contributed to this rich mix. The celebrated cuisine of the Nonyas, a unique liaison of Malay and Chinese cooking, exemplifies the delicious results of this blending of styles. There are also strong influences from Thailand and Indonesia.

Rice forms the basis of the diet of most Malaysians, though noodle dishes are also popular. The characteristic flavours are hot and spicy, and Malay cooks make extensive use of coconut as a basis for curries and soups.

Glossary of popular Malaysian food

- **Satay**: Small pieces of marinated meat, skewered on thin sticks made of coconut-palm ribs, barbecued over charcoal. It is served with spicy peanut sauce, accompanied by slices of cucumber, raw onions and rice cubes (*ketupat*).
- **Gado gado**: Of Indonesian origin, this is a Malaysian salad of cucumber, bean sprouts, fried bean curd and boiled eggs, dressed with spicy peanut sauce.
- **Laksa**: Originated from India, this soupy dish of rice noodles varies from state to state. The soup base is usually flavoured with coconut milk or with tamarind (as in Penang) and served with shredded chicken meat, prawns or fish and bean sprouts.
- **Sambal Belachan**: This is a popular condiment of fermented shrimp paste blended with chillies, garlic and sometimes with lime juice. It is normally eaten with raw vegetables as a sauce (known as *aulam*) or as an accompaniment to other dishes.
- **Roti Chanai**: Of Indian origin, this pancake-like bread is cooked on a hot plate and served with curry. In the preparation of the *roti*, the soft dough is flung in the air

and spun round and round until it stretches into a huge pancake of up to 45cm (18in) in diameter, before it is placed on the hotplate to cook. It is a fascinating sight to watch.

An appetizing display of dishes for an instant lunch in Kota Bharu's Central Market.

• **Bah Kut Teh**: This dish, whose name literally means 'meat bone tea' comes from China. It is made of pork spare ribs stewed with Chinese herbs and garlic, seasoned with soy sauce. There is also a chicken version of this dish, eaten by Muslims. It is a popular breakfast dish.

• **Mee Goreng**: Fried noodles with seafood, meat and vegetables seasoned with soy sauce, this dish is also prepared with rice noodles (vermicelli) or flat white noodles called *koay tiau*, a speciality of hawker stalls in Penang and Ipoh in Perak.

• **Nasi Goreng Istimewa**: Special fried rice with seafood, meat and vegetables served with fried eggs, fried chicken and sometimes satay.

• **Loh Bak**: A speciality of Penang, Chinese in origin, this dish is made of minced pork or chicken, wrapped in beancurd skin and deep fried. Best eaten with chilli sauce.

• **Nasi Lemak**: Coconut rice served with *sambal belachan*, fried peanuts and *ikan bilis* (dried anchovies), boiled egg and sometimes with fried fish. Another popular breakfast dish.

• **Yung Tau Foo**: Clear soup with stuffed beancurd and vegetables, usually served for breakfast.

• **Ais Kachang**: A dessert of shaved ice served with boiled red beans, coconut milk, palm sugar, palm seeds and possibly sweetcorn. Sometimes strips of green jelly are added and the dessert will then be called *cendol*.

• **Air Bandung**: A sweet drink of rose syrup with condensed milk served cold.

THE ART OF TEA-MAKING

Originated from India, *teh tarik* literally means 'pulled tea'. A large spoonful of condensed milk is added to the hot tea in a large beaker and the milky drink is then poured from a great height into another container, in a stream which looks as if it is being 'pulled'. The tea-maker will repeat this incredible task until the tea is frothy. It is served in a glass. The simple reason for 'pulling' the tea is to cool the drink. But Malaysians have transformed this into an entertainment. There are regular competitions amongst veteran tea-makers to determine who can 'pull' the longest tea in tune to music from pop songs.

2
Kuala Lumpur

Kuala Lumpur, the federal capital of Malaysia, is the main gateway to the country. Its name means 'muddy rivermouth' and reflects its humble beginnings as a malaria-infested tin-mining community which grew up at the muddy confluence of two rivers, the **Klang** and the **Gombak**. Historians earmark 1857 as the turning-point for the small mining town. In that year, after an initial disaster when its population of 87 was reduced to less than 20 by malaria, the chief of Klang, Raja Abdullah, rebuilt the community by recruiting another 150 workers. Warehouses, shophouses and shelters for the miners were constructed. Tin-mine prospectors and traders from India, China and even Indonesia flocked to the settlement. The Malays settled in villages upstream from the confluence of the two rivers while the Chinese went downstream and populated the area around today's **Jalan Bandar** and **Jalan Petaling**.

Nineteenth-century Kuala Lumpur was plagued with civil wars spearheaded by local rival rulers. There were further malaria epidemics, fires and violent gang warfare amongst the Chinese. The British, alarmed that the restless situation would lead to a takeover from the Malay rulers, persuaded them to appoint British advisers or Residents at court. The acceptance of a British Resident was tantamount to Selangor becoming a British protectorate and elevated the Resident to a prominence and power previously enjoyed by the Malay chiefs. Under British protection, law and order was restored. The tin mines were re-opened and more rubber plantations

CLIMATE

The temperature in Kuala Lumpur remains between 30° and 33°C (86° and 91°F) all year round, and humidity is high. The buildings retain and reflect the stifling heat, making air-conditioned interiors a welcome relief. There is no distinct rainy or dry season in this area.

The exotic splendour of Kuala Lumpur's Moorish railway station, built by the British in 1910.

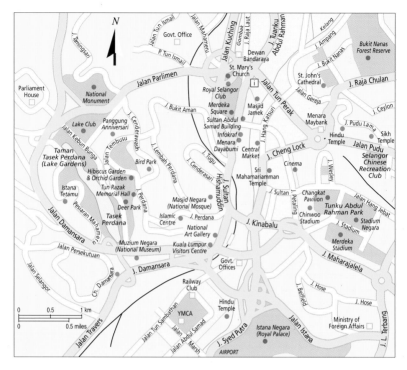

The modern high-rise city of Kuala Lumpur by night.

were established. Against this background, Kuala Lumpur soon became the most important city in Malaya and in 1880 was made the capital of Selangor. In 1974, Kuala Lumpur became a Federal Territory and today is one of the most thriving and prosperous cities in the world, riding on the crest of the economic boom in Malaysia.

A first time visitor to Kuala Lumpur can be forgiven for feeling a little disorientated by the congestion of traffic, the swanky glass skyscrapers, giant department stores and all the confused trappings of any modern city. Yet beneath this veneer of modernity lies the heart and soul of a very interesting metropolis. Tucked into the concrete jungle are the remains of a rich cultural heritage from a bygone era: minareted edifices and handsome colonial buildings, quaint old shophouses in **Chinatown** and **Little India** and suburban Malay *kampungs* (villages). This multicultural society, each community living cheek by jowl with one another and contributing to the flavours and the essence of the country, is typical of every town in Malaysia.

CITY SIGHTSEEING

Sightseeing in Kuala Lumpur (or KL as it is known locally) is an educational experience and needs time to appreciate the sights fully. If the traffic does not, the heat will slow you down anyway.

Merdeka Square ★★★

Merdeka, or Independence, Square is a good starting-point for a tour. A black marble plaque marks the spot where the Union Jack was lowered for the last time at midnight on 30 August 1957 and the Malayan flag hoisted. The national flag today flies on the tallest flagpole in the world, standing at 100m (328ft) at the southern end of the square. This was formerly the ground for cricket, hockey, tennis and rugby matches for the colonial masters, fronting the famous mock-tudor building of the **Selangor Club** which is today strictly for the elite of Kuala Lumpur (with a two-year waiting list for membership).

Stroll across the road to the **Sultan Abdul Samad Building**, built in 1897 to a beautiful Moorish design by the architect A. C. Norman, complete with three copper onion domes and a central clocktower. Once the government administrative centre, it now houses the supreme and high courts. Nearby, beside the Gombak River is **St Mary's Church**, also designed by A. C. Norman. The church has a magnificent pipe organ built by the renowned 19th-century British organ-builder Henry Willis. It is one of Kuala Lumpur's most beautiful old buildings.

DON'T MISS

★★★ The Moorish buildings in the colonial core.
★★ **Masjid Jamek**, the Moghul-style mosque.
★★★ The art deco **Central Market** for art and handicrafts.
★★★ **The National Museum**.
★★★ **The Lake Gardens**, the city's green lung.

The Sultan Abdul Samad Building, previously the State Secretariat, was the first of the Moorish-style public buildings to be erected during the colonial period.

One of Kuala Lumpur's most beautiful buildings, the Masjid Jamek is an oasis of calm in the midst of the bustling city centre.

Masjid Jamek ★★

Further down from the church at the confluence of the Gombak and Klang Rivers is the birthplace of KL where the tin-miners first set up camp in the 1800s and the historic spot is marked by the Masjid Jamek. This architecturally ambitious mosque is Indian Muslim in style with its onion-shaped cupolas, numerous arched colonnades, minarets and balustrades. It was built in 1909 in distinctive stripes of red and white brick, designed by A. C. Norman and A. B. Hubbock.

Infokraf ★★

Along Jalan Raja Laut and Jalan Sultan Hishamuddin, still in the same area, the information centre for Malaysian handicrafts is located in a beautiful renovated Moorish-style building. Arts and crafts from all over Malaysia are displayed together with their cultural background, current research and export potential. It is also a pleasure and a welcome relief from the heat to linger in the air-conditioned room admiring the beautiful batik painting, pottery, handbags, place mats, jewellery and basketwork, all made from local materials. Adjoining Infokraf is the multi-storey complex of **Dayabumi**, the massive white building in Moorish-Byzantine style in keeping with the earlier establishment. It houses the City Point shopping mall, offices and the general post office.

From Dayabumi, an underground passage leads to the **Masjid Negara** – the National Mosque – across the busy road. Built in a modern design incorporating contemporary Islamic art and calligraphy, its outstanding feature is its fan-like roof whose folds and waves symbolize the aspirations of an independent nation. Its 73m (239ft) minaret stands out prominently against the city skyline.

VISITING MOSQUES

It is important to respect the dress code of modesty when visiting a mosque. Women should cover their heads, shoulders and legs; men should wear long trousers. Shoes must always be removed before entering a place of worship.

Kuala Lumpur Railway Station **

Further up Jalan Sultan Hishamuddin, near the Islamic Centre, are perhaps the most famous buildings in KL – the **Railway Station**, built in 1910, and the **Malaya Railway Administration Building** of 1917. Designed once again by the architect A. B. Hubbock, the railway station shows a very strong Moorish influence, featuring domes, arches and minarets which give the majestic appearance of a sultan's palace in the *Arabian Nights* rather than a train station. The British establishment, noted for their attention to detail, delayed the building of the roof until it could meet the specification of the ability to hold up to 1m (3ft) of snow (in the tropical heat?!). The station underwent extensive renovation in 1986, though it now looks a bit frayed at the edges and is undergoing a further facelift, as is the Station Hotel which had also seen better days.

Kuala Lumpur station: a surprising flight of fancy on the part of the British colonial administrators.

The Central Market and Chinatown ***

Backtracking a little down the road across the Klang River is Kuala Lumpur's equivalent of London's Covent Garden – the **Central Market** (Pasar Seni) – an art deco building of 1936 and formerly a 'wet' market selling fish, meat and vegetables. It is now a delightful, vibrant place selling arts and crafts from Malaysia, Thailand, the Philippines and Indonesia. The market has 130 shops, 30 food outlets, 140 small stalls, cinemas, an exhibition corner (Sudut Pameran) and an outdoor riverside amphitheatre staging free cultural performances. Prices for goods here are fixed and bargaining is not encouraged. This is a good place to shop for bric-à-brac.

A short distance away is Jalan Petaling, the heart of KL's **Chinatown**, reflecting the important role the

Striking souvenirs of your visit to Malaysia can be found on the numerous stalls of KL's Central Market.

A Chinese artist working in traditional style in his shop in the Central Market, Kuala Lumpur.

Chinese play in Malaysian society. Trading starts early in the morning, before the onslaught of the peak hours. There are vendors selling seafood, fruits and vegetables while the shops, dating back as far as the 1900s, sell an array of oriental goods ranging from dried duck, Chinese sausages, mushrooms and traditional medicine to gold and ironmongery. There are coffee shops and roadside stalls selling roast duck, pork, chicken, noodles, herbal soup and local delicacies. By night, the whole street is closed to traffic and transformed into a bustling market-place selling a mind-boggling selection of fake designer goods, video tapes of the latest film releases, Russian army surplus binoculars and radios (which weigh a ton), T-shirts, clothes and jewellery. This is the liveliest shopping area in KL and brings out the real excitement of shopping in Malaysia.

Sri Mahamariamman ★★

A few minutes from Chinatown, this Hindu temple is a colourful and ornate building full of decorative features and intricate carvings of Hindu deities. Shoes must be removed before entering the temple and for 20 sens you can leave your footwear in a pigeon-hole in a shop next door for safe-keeping. The temple was founded in 1873 and is said to be the most ornate and elaborate in the country.

The Lake Gardens ★★★

The city's green spaces open out a little further away from the centre. The Lake Gardens (Taman Tasek Perdana) near Jalan Parlimen were constructed in the 1880s. The park has 92ha (230 acres) of lush greenery, with flowering shrubs and trees around an artificial lake. On a hilltop within the gardens is the Orchid Garden, featuring over 800 species, and a Hibiscus Garden with 500 varieties in every shape and colour. Admission is free except on Saturday, Sunday, public holidays and

---

THE ART OF HAGGLING

In Malaysia's bustling markets, haggling and bargaining are the order of the day. One must never pay the price the seller asks for. Having enquired the price of your chosen article, always put on an act of a little reservation and do not show too much eagerness to buy if you want the best bargain. Sometimes prices can be lowered by as much as 50%!

Colourful little boats await the crowds in Kuala Lumpur's Lake Gardens. The gardens provide a green escape from the heat of the city centre, and are a popular venue for joggers and picnickers, though they started life as a botanic garden with the aim of developing new crops for the colonial planters.

exhibition days when there is a small charge for adults. The garden is open from 09:00 to 18:30. There is a shuttle service to take you round the park. Opposite the orchid garden is the Bird Park where exotic species of birds from all over the world are kept in spacious landscaped gardens enclosed in wire netting. A unique feature is the hornbill enclosure where giant rhinoceros hornbills with bright orange casques fly freely, dive-bombing visitors and frequenting the Carl's Junior Restaurant situated in the park. Diners can observe the hornbills from the comforts of the dining-room. The Bird Park is open from 08:00 to 18:00 daily.

Malaysia Butterfly Park **

Between 8000 and 10,000 live butterflies of 150 species fly freely here amongst 15,000 plants of 100 different species which have been used to create as closely as possible the natural habitat of the butterflies. You can watch the pupae turning into butterflies before your very eyes. There are also artificially constructed waterfalls, tortoise ponds, an exotic insects corner, rabbits and guinea pigs, while seed-feeding finches fly freely amongst the butterflies. Opening times are 09:00 to 17:00 on weekdays and 09:00 to 18:00 at weekends and on public holidays. There is an entrance charge, plus a further charge of RM1.00 if you want to take your camera into the park to take pictures.

HORNBILLS

Hornbills are Malaysia's most striking birds and the largest is the rhinoceros hornbill. Their wingbeats make a distinctive noise which some people compare to the puffing of a steam train. Their honking call is also unmistakable.

The birds are usually seen in pairs and apparently mate for life. The female nests in a tree-hole, into which she is sealed by the male who plasters her in with a mixture of mud, grass and saliva. She remains imprisoned for about three months until her single chick is old enough to fly, and during this time her tireless mate feeds her through a narrow slit in the mud wall, just big enough for her bill.

National Monument *

Across the road from the Lake Gardens, this memorial was constructed in 1966 in honour of the nation's war heroes. Sculpted by the American Felix de Weldon, who also designed the Iwo Jima Memorial in Washington, the bronze monument, 15.5m (51ft) high, depicts seven men from the Malayan Security Forces, symbolizing the seven qualities of leadership. The imposing sculpture is surrounded by fountains and a moat filled with water-lilies.

National Museum ***

To the south of the Lake Gardens at Jalan Damansara, the museum is built in the style of old Malay architecture. It is a treasure-house of exhibits on local history, culture and traditions, arts and crafts, economic activities, native flora and fauna, weapons and currency. In the grounds are locomotives, vintage cars and other transportation of bygone eras. There are reconstructions of Malay palaces from other parts of the country. It is an excellent introduction to Malaysia's history. The museum also holds special exhibitions of specific aspects of life and culture from other parts of the world. Admission is free but there is a small charge for the special exhibitions. It opens daily from 09:00 to 18:00.

Thean Hou Temple **

On a hilltop overlooking Jalan Syed Putra, this magnificent Chinese temple is one of the largest in the Far East. Looking like a grand emperor's palace, it has a golden roof with dragons perched on the eaves, and imposing red pillars supporting the whitewashed structure. Statues of mythological figures and deities stand guard in the grounds. In a small garden by the side of the temple is a 'hi-tech' statue of the Goddess of Mercy which spouts holy water when a devotee kneels in front of her. Plastic cups are provided to receive this water for drinking. Shoes must be removed before entering the main praying hall. Nearby is **Istana Negara**, the official residence of the King of Malaysia. The palace was once the mansion of a tin magnate.

An ornate altar in the Thean Hou Chinese temple.

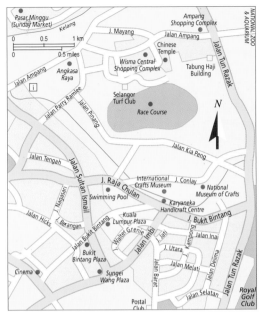

JALAN AMPANG

Once the homes of the early tin magnates of Kuala Lumpur, the grandiose mansions along this leafy road now house many embassies and consulates. **Le Coq d'Or** at 121 Jalan Ampang (recommended for its European and Malaysian cuisine) was built in 1919 by a Chinese tin miner whose will stipulated that the house should not be altered in any way. Consequently, its crumbling splendour exudes the atmosphere of the colonial era.

Crafts Museums

The **Karyaneka Handicraft Centre** in Jalan Raja Chulan provides for one-stop souvenir shopping, selling arts and crafts from all over Malaysia. In the same vicinity is the **National Museum of Crafts**, displaying traditional works of art by local craftsmen in ceramics, brass and silverware. Behind the Karyaneka complex is the **International Crafts Museum** and next to the museum is Taman Karyaneka, an ethno-botanical garden featuring plants from various parts of the country.

Malaysia Tourist Information Centre

In Jalan Ampang, the **Malaysia Tourist Information Centre** (MATIC) has an exhibition hall, information counter, souvenir shops, a restaurant and travel services. Cultural performances and audio-visual shows are held daily. This beautiful colonial building, dating from 1935, was formerly the mansion of a Malayan planter and tin-miner. It served as the British Army headquarters in 1941.

Mengkuang, *or palm leaf weaving, is used to make a wide variety of household articles.*

The hundreds of shops and stalls in the Central Market are a great place to browse.

A BARGAIN-HUNTER'S DREAM

Kuala Lumpur is a shopper's paradise where all imaginable kinds of goods are available, mostly at bargain prices. However, imported European designer goods like handbags, clothes, shoes and other branded items, especially cosmetics, can be more expensive than in the West. Goods from the Far East, especially Korea, Taiwan and Hong Kong, and local products, are very good value for money and are usually of good quality. Electrical goods are also very competitive. Whether it is an exotic oriental treasure you are seeking, a silk batik shirt or local handicrafts, shopping in Kuala Lumpur is an exciting and often rewarding experience when you can snap up a bargain at half the price you are accustomed to paying elsewhere. For those who have gold credit cards to wave about, there are some very exclusive stores to browse in.

Royal Selangor Pewter Factory ★★

Pewter, an alloy of pure tin with a small proportion of copper and antimony for added strength, is one of Malaysia's most famous products. The art of pewtermaking was brought to the country by a Chinese immigrant, Yong Koon, who used traditional methods to produce handcrafted ceremonial and domestic pewterware for his wealthy clientele. The industry began in 1885 following the discovery of abundant tin ore in the Larut region in Perak and in Kuala Lumpur. At the factory a guide will take you through the various processes involved in the making of pewterware. All items are painstakingly handcrafted to the finest detail. The tour inevitably ends at the showroom where you may purchase the finished product. The factory is at 4 Jalan Usahawan Enam, Setapak Jaya, on the outskirts of Kuala Lumpur, and is open Monday to Saturday (including public holidays) from 08:00 to 16:45 and on Sunday from 09:00 to 16:00. The factory has showrooms in most department stores in central KL.

SHOPPING
Jalan Bukit Bintang/Jalan Sultan Ismail/Jalan Imbi

Many of the famous department stores are situated here in 'The Golden Triangle' of Kuala Lumpur. **Metrojaya** at BB Plaza is a huge store offering mid-range to up-market clothes and accessories, shoes, handbags, cosmetics, toys and household goods. There are various independent concessions within the store selling books, computer wares and electrical goods.

Sungei Wang Plaza comprises many small outlets selling leisure wear, sports gear, optical products, shoes, handbags and watches, and is popular with the local people. Prices of goods here are very reasonable and bargaining is allowed. It also has several food outlets selling mainly hawker-style meals and snacks. It is a good place to shop for clothes and some shops offer an instant alteration service for clothing that needs adjustment.

Parkson Grand offers fashion wear, handbags, cosmetics, toys and household goods while **Imbi Plaza** is the place for computers and their peripherals. **Lot 10**, opposite Sungei Wang on Jalan Bukit Bintang, linked by a covered pedestrian bridge, is leased by **Isetan** and offers mid-range to expensive goods. The top floor of the store is devoted to exclusive designer clothes. Also on the same road is **Kuala Lumpur Plaza** which specializes in top-of-the-range watches, travel goods, handbags, shoes and fashionable jewellery. At Jalan Ampang/Jalan Tun Razak, the **Yow Chuan Plaza** and **City Square** are two stores for up-market goods and a good place for antiques and souvenir collectors. The **Ampang Park Shopping Complex** has many boutiques, fashion houses, jewellery shops, electrical and electronic goods.

For handicrafts, antiques, curios and works of art, the **Central Market, Infokraf** and **Karyaneka** offer a wide choice. **Chinatown** in Jalan Petaling is a bargain hunters' paradise selling inexpensive clothes and imitation watches and bags. There are also many shops and department stores at Jalan Tuanku Abdul Rahman, a curious blend of ultramodern buildings sandwiched between pre-war shophouses which have been caringly restored.

Kuala Lumpur at a Glance

KL is not affected by the monsoon from Oct–Mar, but gets consistent rainfall between Apr–Sep. Merdeka (Independence) Day is 31 Aug, with festivals, parades, lights and decorations. Followed by Malaysia Fest which usually runs throughout Sep, with cultural shows, exhibitions, food festivals, sports and traditional games.

Subang International Airport is 24km (15 miles) from KL. There are taxis and limousine services into the city. Prepay the fare by buying a voucher at the airport, stating destination, to avoid being overcharged. Tipping the driver is not encouraged. Three bus companies operate buses to downtown KL: some are air-conditioned.

Metered taxis can be hailed by the roadside or from taxi stands. Taxi drivers in the city centre quite often refuse to take passengers if there is a traffic jam especially during rush hour (07:30 – 09:00 and 17:00 – 18:30). It might be faster to walk in any case: traffic can take two hours to travel a mile!

The pink minibuses charge a standard fare for any destination; omnibuses charge a flag-down fare and a further fare that varies with the distance travelled.

Luxury
Hotel Istana, 73 Jl Raja Chulan, tel (03) 241 9988;
The Regent of Kuala Lumpur, 160, Jl Bukit Bintang, tel (03) 241 8000;
Shangri-la Hotel, 11, Jl Sultan Ismail, tel (03) 232 2388;
Kuala Lumpur Hilton, Jl Sultan Ismail, tel (03) 248 2322.
Concorde Hotel, 2 Jl Sultan Ismail, tel (03) 244 2200;
Equatorial Hotel, Jl Sultan Ismail, tel (03) 261 7777;
Park Royal, Jl Sultan Ismail, tel (03) 242 5588;
Crown Princess, Jl Tun Razak, tel (03) 262 5522;
Holiday Inn on the Park, Jl Pinang, tel (03) 248 1066.
Mid-range
The Plaza Hotel, Jl Raja Laut, tel (03) 298 2255;
Hotel Grand Continental, Jl Belia, tel (03) 292 9333;
Hotel Malaysia, 67-69 Jl Bukit Bintang, tel (03) 242 8033;
Hotel Grand Pacific, Jl Tun Ismail, tel (03) 442 2177;
Budget
Sungei Wang Hotel, 74-76 Jl Bukit Bintang, tel (03) 248 5255;
Apollo Hotel, 106-110, Jl Bukit Bintang, tel (03) 242 8133;
Hotel Malaysia, Jl Bukit Bintang, tel (03) 242 8033
The Lodge, 2, Jl Tengah, tel (03) 242 0122.
YMCA of Kuala Lumpur, Jl Tun Sambanthan, tel (03) 274 1439;
Central Hotel, 510 Jl Tuanku Abdul Rahman, tel (03) 442 2981;
Colonial Hotel, 29-45 Jl Sultan, tel (03) 238 0336;
Malaysian Youth Hostels Association, 21 Jl Kampong Atap, tel (03) 230 6870.
Diamond City Lodge, 74B, C,D, Jl Masjid India, tel (03) 203 2245;
Lodge 51, 51 Jl Ampang, tel (03) 232 4673;
Paradise Bed and Breakfast, 319-1, Jl Tuanku Abdul Rahman, tel (03) 293 2322.

Food at hawkers' stalls can cost as little as RM3.00 for a bowl of noodles. The average price for a good three course meal in KL will be about RM40.00 for a party of four in ordinary restaurants. Don't let the less salubrious-looking places put you off as they tend to produce the best food.

Restaurants serving Malay food with cultural performances in the evening:
Eden Village, 260 Jl Raja Chulan, tel (03) 241 4027: best known for seafood;
Nelayan Floating Restaurant, Titiwangsa Lake Gardens, tel (03) 422 8600;
Seri Melayu, Jl Conlay (near the KL Hilton), tel (03) 245 1833: extensive buffet;
Yazmin, 6 Jl Kia Peng, tel (03) 241 5655.

Kuala Lumpur at a Glance

Indian
Bangles Restaurant, 60-A Jl Tuanku Abdul Rahman, tel (03) 298 6770;
Bilal Restaurant, 33 Jl Ampang, tel (03) 238 0804;
Devi Annapoorna Restaurant (vegetarian), 94 Lorong Maarof, tel (03) 255 6443;
Devi's, Brickfields, Jl Tun Sambanthan (famous for banana leaf dishes);
Mitra Kanchana Curry & Tandoori, 237G Jl Tun Sambanthan, Brickfields, tel (03) 273 4153;
Shiraz, 1 Jl Medan Tuanku.
Chinese
Futt Yow Yuen (vegetarian), 9 Jl Balai Polis, tel (03) 238 5704;
Hakka Restaurant, 231 Jl Bukit Bintang, tel (03) 985 8492: braised meat dishes;
Lee Wong Kee, 239 Jl Tuanku Abdul Rahman, tel (03) 291 2606;
Restoran Sze Chuan, 42-3 Jl Sultan Ismail, tel (03) 242 7083: spicy Szechuan food;
Woo Lam by Jl Tun Sambanthan under flyover. Off tourist track and crowded with locals.
Hotel restaurants
Dondang Sayang Restoran (Malay/Nonya), Ming Court Hotel, Jl Ampang, tel (03) 261 8888;
Shang Palace (Chinese), Shangri-la Hotel, Jl Sultan Ismail, tel (03) 232 2388;
Sawasdee Thai Restaurant, Holiday Inn on the Park, tel (03) 248 1066;

Spices, Concorde Hotel, Jl Sultan Ismail, tel (03) 244 2200. Malaysian, Nonya, Moghul, Thai and Indonesian dishes;
Taj Restaurant (Indian), Crown Princess Hotel, Jl Tun Razak, tel (03) 262 5522;
Restaurants serving Western and Eastern food
Bon Ton, 7 Jl Kia Peng, tel (03) 241 3614: old colonial bungalow in city centre;
Coliseum Café, Jl Tuanku Abdul Rahman, tel 292 6270. Old colonial restaurant complete with original grime. Famous for sizzling steaks cooked at the table;
East West Kopitiam, 2nd Floor, Sungei Wang Plaza, Jl Sultan Ismail, tel (03) 248 4289;
The Ship, 102-4 Jl Bukit Bintang, tel (03) 244 3605.

TOURS AND EXCURSIONS

Daytime **city tours** of major places of interest usually last about 3 hours. **Evening tours** take in Jl Petaling (Chinatown) and night market at Kampung Baru (liveliest on Sat).
Day trips to Batu Caves, batik and pewter factories, hill resorts, Melaka, Negeri Sembilan, and many others.

Excursions can be booked through most hotels, or local travel companies such as:
Babin Tours, Wisma Concorde, tel (03) 248 0888;
DIS Travel & Tours, Lot 213, 2nd Floor, Kompleks Antarabangsa, Jl Sultan Ismail, tel (03) 242 9246;
Mayflower Acme Tours, 18 Jl Segambut Pusat, tel (03) 626 7011;
Nanda Tours & Travel, Bang Dato Zainal, tel (03) 298 6131.

USEFUL CONTACTS

Malaysian Tourism Promotion Board, 17, 24th-27th Floor, Menara Dato' Onn, Putra World Trade Centre, 45, Jl Tun Dr Ismail, tel (03) 293 5188;
Malaysia Tourist Information Centre (MATIC), Jl Ampang, tel (03) 242 3929;
Kuala Lumpur Tourist Information Centre, Jl Parlimen, tel (03) 293 6664;
National Library of Malaysia, Jl Tun Razak, tel (03) 293 3488;
Car Rental Association of KL & Selangor, 40 Jl Sultan Ismail, tel (03) 241 0561.

KUALA LUMPUR	J	F	M	A	M	J	J	A	S	O	N	D
AVERAGE TEMP. °F	78	80	80	80	80	80	80	80	78	78	78	78
AVERAGE TEMP. °C	26	27	27	27	27	27	27	27	26	26	26	26
Hours of Sun Daily	6	6	7	7	7	6	7	6	5	6	5	5
RAINFALL in	6	6	9	11	7	5	5	6	8	11	11	9
RAINFALL mm	162	144	218	284	183	126	129	145	192	272	275	230
Days of Rainfall	10	11	14	16	13	9	10	11	13	17	18	15

3
Beyond Kuala Lumpur

Kuala Lumpur is a good starting-point for excursions to a variety of outstanding places of interest. Within a few hours' drive are the cool hill resorts of Cameron Highlands, Fraser's Hill and Genting Highlands, the awe-inspiring Hindu cave temple at Batu Caves or a journey back in time to the historic city of Melaka.

Batu Caves **

The famous Batu Caves lie north of Kuala Lumpur in the direction of Ipoh, in the state of Perak. A 45-minute drive, turning off the main road, brings you to a massive limestone outcrop which is honeycombed with a series of caves. One of the biggest in the system is the Cathedral Cave, deriving its name from its towering stalactites and stalagmites. The huge cavern was transformed into a Hindu temple in 1891, and is reached by climbing 272 steps. At the start of the climb visitors walk over a small flame to undergo a symbolic spiritual cleansing before entering the temple. Statues of deities from the Hindu pantheon are erected in colourfully painted shrines. Worshippers come daily to make offerings of coconuts, fruits, milk and flowers. The temple has a menagerie of turkeys, chickens, monkeys, cats and pigeons all roaming freely, given sanctuary by the temple as the Hindus have a deep respect for animals. Visitors feed them with green beans, coconuts and bananas.

The temple is dedicated to the Hindu god, Lord Murugan (otherwise known as Lord Subramaniam), and

CLIMATE

The temperate climate of the hill resorts is the perfect antidote to the constant heat and humidity of the lowlands. Fraser's Hill and Cameron Highlands enjoy daytime temperatures around 20°C (68°F), dropping to 10°C (50°F) in the evening, when clouds envelop the hilltops and log fires are lit.

Opposite: *Tea bushes cloak the rolling hills of the Cameron Highlands. The first plantations were established in the 1920s.*

DON'T MISS

** **Batu Caves**: Site of the
spectacular festival of
Thaipusam in January or
February.
** **The Hill Resorts**: The
essential cool retreat from
the city.
*** **Melaka**: The historic city
of the Malay sultanate.

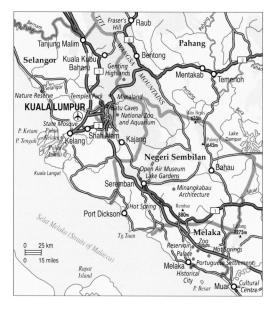

*Stalactites silhouetted
against the daylight at the
entrance to the Batu Caves.*

is the setting for the spectacular annual celebration of
Thaipusam (see page 26). At the foot of the temple there
are several souvenir shops, vegetarian restaurants and
stalls selling drinks, which are much needed after the
hike of 272 steps each way.
Fortune-tellers abound to
predict your future: they
will charge RM10.00 for
palm-reading or RM2.00
for a mini version of your
future told with the aid of
a tarot card picked at ran-
dom by a bird, usually a
parakeet or a canary.

Shah Alam (Selangor) ★★
After Kuala Lumpur
became a Federal Territory
in 1974, the sultan of
Selangor built a new state

The Selangor State Mosque at Shah Alam is the biggest in Malaysia and can accommodate 16,000 worshippers under one of the largest domes in the world.

capital. The border between the two territories is marked by an ornate Malaysian-style gate with domes and minarets. The city is Shah Alam and it is dominated by industries and big companies. Its main attraction is the magnificent **Shah Alam Mosque**, completed in 1988, the largest mosque in Southeast Asia, with its sparkling turquoise dome and four towering minarets standing guard on each corner.

About fifteen's minute drive away is the **Malaysia Agriculture Park** (Bukit Cahaya Sri Alam), one of the first agro-forestry parks in the world. Opened in 1986, its permanent displays occupy a site of 1258ha (3110 acres) against a backdrop of lush tropical jungle. Visitors can watch the entire process of *padi* (rice) cultivation, or take a walk through the Spice and Beverage Garden, where cinnamon, cloves, pepper, tea and exotic spices and herbs evoke Malaysia's rich history as a key producer of the best of these condiments, luring traders, colonial powers and explorers to its shores. Stroll through the Orchid Gardens and revel in the vibrant profusion of flowers of wild species and cultivated varieties. Other attractions include the Cocoa Gardens, Mushroom Garden, an Aviary Park, Animal Park, Four Seasons Temperate House depicting the annual cycle, and a stocked lake where visitors can fish. There are recreational areas for picnics and jungle treks, as well as a handicraft centre - in fact there is something for everyone.

DANCE OF THE FIREFLY

For a really 'glittering' experience if you have an evening to spare, take a trip to Kuala Selangor, a small town at the mouth of the Selangor River. The journey from KL takes about two hours. At night, near the tiny village of Kampung Kuantan at Batang Berjuntai, millions of fireflies light up the mangrove swamp along the river-bank like a Christmas tree. For this nocturnal safari a village boatman will row you up the river in a small boat (it will hold four people) to admire the spectacular sight. Complete silence should be observed and flash photography and smoking are not permitted. Life jackets must be worn. As this is not a very touristy place and difficult to find at night, it is best to travel with a local tour operator. For details, contact DIS Travel, Lot 213, 2nd Floor, Kompleks Antarabangsa, Jalan Sultan Ismail, 50250 Kuala Lumpur, tel (03) 2429246, fax (03) 2421771.

THE HILL RESORTS
Genting Highlands *

An hour's drive from Kuala Lumpur, 2000m (6560ft) above sea level, is the gambling capital of Malaysia, Genting Highlands. It is a sophisticated resort, like a mini 'Las Vegas in the clouds'. The casino has Western as well as Chinese gaming tables. Gamblers must be smartly dressed with ties or in the formal Malaysian attire of long-sleeved batik shirts. For non-gamblers, there is an 18-hole golf course at the **Awana Golf and Country Club**, with over 45ha (110 acres) of challenging landscape. The cable-car ride will afford you a splendid view of the virgin forest below as it travels from 914m (3000 ft) to 1768m (5800ft) up the mountain. For entertainment there is a theatre-restaurant serving Chinese food with lavish shows performed by international artistes and dance troupes. There are several hotels and apartments available for holidaymakers.

Fraser's Hill **

North-east of Kuala Lumpur, 99km (62 miles) away, is the hill resort of Fraser's Hill, actually built on seven hills, 1524m (5000ft) above sea level. Named after Louis James Fraser, an intrepid trader with interests in tin, opium and gambling, it has a very colonial atmosphere

Montane rainforest seen from Fraser's Hill, with the thickly forested slopes of the Banjaran Titiwangsa in the background.

with its bungalows and gardens. It is rich in wildlife and even tigers have been known to make a rare appearance. The narrow winding road has an alternate one-way system on an hourly basis over the last 8km (5 miles) between 06:30 and 19:00. There are several hotels, bungalows and chalets available for visitors, including the **Merlin Resort**, the biggest hotel there, which overlooks the golf course.

Cameron Highlands **

Straddling the states of Perak and Pahang is the best-known hill station in Malaysia, the Cameron Highlands. Named after William Cameron, a government surveyor who explored the area in 1885, the resort nestles amongst sweeping valleys and mountains. At 1524m (5000ft) above sea level it enjoys a refreshingly cool climate, with temperatures no higher than 20°C (68°F) and rarely falling below 10°C (50°F). Here flowers, fruits and vegetables grow in profusion, not to mention the rolling green carpet of the tea plantations. The Orang Asli, the indigenous peoples of Peninsular Malaysia, lead a semi-nomadic life in the highland forest, building small *atap* huts on the hill slopes. They are slowly being integrated into Malaysian society and some have found employment in the area. It is possible to stop at one of these settlements on the way to watch them making bamboo traps and baskets. For a small fee they will demonstrate their skill at blowpipe shooting. If you wish to photograph them, it is only polite to ask for permission first.

Ringlet, a small town with shops and hotels, stands guard at the bottom of the hill before reaching Cameron Highlands proper. You may want to stop at **Lata Iskander**, a beautiful waterfall by the roadside halfway up to the Highlands. The air cools by degrees as you travel further to **Tanah Rata** and **Brinchang**, the two Highlands towns. Both have plenty of accommodation, shops, restaurants, fruit and flower stalls selling the local produce. The fruit and vegetables here taste better and sweeter than in the lowlands, and grow to prodigious size: some cauliflowers are as big as footballs! The popu-

STEAMBOAT

Cameron Highlands is renowned for its steamboat, not the type you sail in but the kind you eat. Steamboat is a famous Chinese dish not unlike the European fondue, except that in this case the food is cooked in steaming soup. Pieces of raw fish, seafood, meat, chicken, vegetables and noodles are arranged on the table with various sauces for dips. Diners place the raw food in the soup and after a few bubbling minutes, the food is ready to eat. Each person is equipped with a small wire ladle with which to scoop the morsels out of the boiling soup. The soup is, of course, at its best at the end of the meal when all the flavours of the food are mingled in it. This is the time to add the noodles for a really delicious finale. In the cool Cameron air, this is just the tonic to get you going!

Ye Olde Smokehouse, overlooking the golf course in Tanah Rata, was built fifty years ago by a British resident of the Cameron Highlands, Stanley Foster. Its original style has been carefully preserved by the present management.

OLD ENGLAND IN THE HEART OF MALAYSIA

At the top of the range of accommodation in the Highlands, and oozing old colonial charm, is Ye Olde Smokehouse Country House Hotel. Built like a Tudor mansion and set in a beautiful garden, the hotel has latticed windows, wooden beams, comfortable armchairs and working fireplaces. The restaurant serves typical English cuisine like steak and kidney pies and roast beef with Yorkshire pudding. There are even Devonshire cream teas with freshly baked scones in the afternoon. There are no telephones in the bedrooms and guests have to go out into the garden to use the British red telephone box (now nearly extinct in Britain) to make a call. Most bedrooms have four-poster beds to complete the effect.

lation is predominantly Chinese who make their living as farmers. Every piece of land is cultivated, with vegetables and fruit grown on terraces carved into the hills.

No visit to this resort is complete without a trip to the tea plantations. The most famous plantations belong to **Boh Tea**, the first highland estate in the country, established in 1929 by John Archibald Russell. The company has two estates, one at each end of the Highlands, the Boh Tea Estate in the south near Ringlet and the Sungai Palas Tea Estate near Gunung Brinchang in the northernmost part of Cameron Highlands. Both plantations are still owned by the Russell family and produce 4 million kilograms (3940 tons) of tea per year. You will be invited to watch the production of tea from the time it is picked to the end product, as it goes through archaic machines, driers, rollers and giant sieves to produce one of the finest teas in the world.

Other attractions in the area include a butterfly farm (though not as impressive as the one in KL, it has a large collection of Rajah Brooke's birdwing butterflies), rose gardens, flower nurseries and the Sam Poh Kong Buddhist temple at Brinchang. For the adventurous traveller, jungle treks are organized by local tour operators. Cameron Highlands may have lost a few of its old charms through the onslaught of tourism, but the rolling hills, the green terraces of vegetables and the spectacular valleys of the tea plantations will make your visit really worthwhile.

Negeri Sembilan

Wedged between KL and Melaka is the 'State of Nine Districts'. The traditions of its early settlers, the Minangkabau from Sumatra, included a matriarchal system: women play an important part in society and traditionally inherited a major portion of the family wealth. It is famous for its fiery dishes spiced with *cilli padi* (very hot small chilli) and *lemang* – glutinous rice cooked in bamboo stems. The outstanding buffalo-horn roofs of Minangkabau architecture dominate most of the landscape (even the petrol stations are built in this style).

Seremban *

The state capital is 64km (40 miles) from KL and makes an easy day trip. Once a two-shophouse tin-mining centre, it has developed into a busy town with shopping complexes and international standard hotels. The **State Assembly Building** is in the Minangkabau style, and doubles as a venue for state assemblies and the town library.

The beautiful **Lake Gardens**, with two lakes and a collection of plants found in the country, is a favourite with locals and health enthusiasts who use the park for jogging and to practise Tai Chi. A floating stage on one of the lakes is used for cultural shows at the weekend.

Taman Seni Budaya is a cultural complex at Labur Spur. Three outstanding historical buildings are located here. The **Terapak Perpatih** is a Minangkabau building which houses handicrafts, costumes and weapons, and the **Istana Ampang Tinggi** (State Museum) was formerly a royal residence built in 1861. The third building is the beautifully carved **Rumah Minangkabau**, also known as Rumah Hantu (the Haunted House) by the locals because of its gloomy appearance. It was constructed in 1898 for a Malay prince and was taken to England in 1924 for an exhibition as an example of Malay architecture. The interior is not open to the public.

Port Dickson **

Situated 32km (20 miles) from Seremban, Port Dickson is a popular seaside resort for Malaysians, particularly during weekends and holidays. It has 18km (11 miles) of white sandy beaches stretching from **Tanjung Gemuk** in the north to **Tanjung Tuan** in the south. Windsurfers and water-skiers abound here, while the stretch of beach called the **Blue Lagoon** is ideal for deep-sea diving. There are chalets and bungalows for hire as well as hotels in the area.

SRI MENANTI

Some 30km (19 miles) east of Seremban is the old Minangkabau capital of Negeri Sembilan. The Istana Lama Sri Menanti, originally the residence of the head of state, is a beautiful Minangkabau wooden palace dating from 1908, with a sweeping shingle roof and intricate carving on the walls and verandahs. It is now a museum housing weaponry and traditional bridal costumes, with a bridal chamber and wedding dais.

MELAKA

Two hours' journey south of Kuala Lumpur, 147km (91 miles) away, is the historic town of Melaka on the west coast of Malaysia. This was the centre of the Malay Sultanate in the 15th century. It was founded by a refugee Sumatran prince, Parameswara, who is said to have named the town after the *melaka* tree under which he stopped to rest. During its heyday it was a thriving port trading in gold, silk, tea, opium, tobacco, perfumes, spices and other commodities from neighbouring countries and as far away as Europe and South America. Melaka reached the peak of its supremacy during the reign of Sultan Mansur Shah, who ruled from 1459 to 1477. The importance of this town, particularly its role in the spice trade, prompted the Portuguese, the Dutch and the British successively to colonize the port. Each colonial regime left behind a legacy which today provides historical interest on the tourist circuit of attractions.

Visiting Melaka on a day trip does not do this fascinating city any justice. To appreciate the real flavour of the place and savour the atmosphere, not to mention the tantalizing Nonya cuisine, a three day/two night stay is recommended. Most of the historic sights of Melaka are within walking distance of one another.

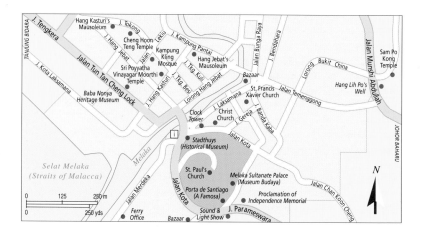

Historical Square ***

The bright red **Stadthuys** (Townhouse) was built in 1650 as the official residence of the Dutch governors and their officers. It is now the **Musium Sejarah** (or Historical Museum) where some authentic Portuguese and Dutch relics as well as traditional Chinese and Malay costumes are displayed. It opens daily from 09:00 to 18:00 except on Fridays when it is closed between 12:15 and 14:45 to allow Muslims to observe the rites of the holy day. Next to the Stadthuys is **Christ Church**, which was completed in 1753. It is an excellent example of Dutch architecture. A notable feature of the church is its ceiling, whose beams, over 15m (16yd) long, were each made from a single tree. The 200-year-old pews all survive. Over the altar there is a painting of the Last Supper on glazed tiles and on the floors are tombstones in Armenian script. Entry to the church is free but you are politely asked to make an optional donation towards its upkeep. Further up the road, next to the Malaysian Youth Museum, is **St Francis Xavier's Church** which was built in 1849 by a French priest, the Reverend Farve. This Gothic church is dedicated to St Francis Xavier who was a missionary in Southeast Asia during the 16th Century.

On the hilltop site of the former Melakan sultan's palace, is the ruin of **St Paul's Church**. It was built by a Portuguese captain, Duarte Coelho, in 1521, when it was called 'Our Lady of the Anunciation' and known as 'Our Lady of the Hill'. When the Protestant Dutch assumed power in Melaka, they changed the dedication. The body of St Francis Xavier was briefly enshrined here in 1553 before being shipped to Goa in India. Today the empty

The distinctive red buildings of Dutch colonial Melaka. On the left is the façade of Christ Church, built in 1753, and on the right, the older Stadthuys, built on the foundations of the old Portuguese fort.

THE MALAY ANNALS

The opulent Melakan court of the 15th century is vividly evoked in a contemporary history of the sultanate known as the *Sejarah Melayu*, which is acknowledged to be the finest work of literature in the Malay language. It was translated into English by C. C. Brown in 1953 (revised edition, Oxford University Press, Kuala Lumpur, 1970).

Above: *The Porta de Santiago, all that remains of the huge Portuguese fortress that once covered the whole of St Paul's Hill.*

Opposite: *A nineteenth-century lighthouse, built by the British, stands in front of the ruins of St Paul's Church. To the left is a marble memorial to St Francis Xavier, erected in 1953.*

grave remains open in the church. The Dutch used the church as a fortress and burial ground for their noble dead: huge granite tombstones of the Dutch and the British remain in the grounds of the church-yard today.

From the church, a number of steps will lead you down to the site of **A Famosa**, the massive fortress built by the Portuguese in 1511. During the skirmish between the Dutch and the Portuguese in 1641, much of the building was damaged but the Dutch restored it in 1670. When Melaka was handed over to Britain, the British began to demolish the fortress, until the intervention of Sir Stamford Raffles, the founder of Singapore. He managed to save only the gateway, how-ever. The **Porta de Santiago** remains as the only material legacy of the Portuguese era. Next to the fortress is the reconstruction of the 15th-century **Melakan Sultanate's Palace**, built from the original plan of an ancient palace found in the Malay historical chronicle, the *Sejarah Melayu*. It serves as the Melaka Cultural Museum dis-playing the splendour of the sultans' lifestyle including a royal bedchamber.

Opposite the Palace Museum is the **Historic City Memorial Garden** with a strong Islamic theme focusing on the monument commemorating the declaration of Melaka as an Historic City on 15 April 1989. Next to the memorial garden is the **Proclamation of Independence Memorial**, a Dutch colonial building which formerly housed the Malacca Club, the social centre of the British colonial era. It now contains an exhibition illustrating events leading to Malaysian independence.

Heritage Trail ★★★

Moving away from the historic square, a ten-minute taxi ride (or twenty minutes by rickshaw) will take you to **Jalan Tun Tan Cheng Lock** (known as 'Millionaire's Row' and formerly called Heeren Street), a narrow street lined with ancient shophouses that still evoke the good old days of the wealthy Baba/Nonya community. This is the old part of the city. The shophouses have a 'five-foot way' forming a walkway in front, which leads to tall wooden doors and shuttered windows painted in charmingly faded colours. Most of the façades of these townhouses are decorated with beautiful tile motifs and delicate carvings of flowers and birds. Some of the houses are in need of repair but the semi-dilapidated state of the buildings only adds to the air of history and authenticity that pervades this part of the city. On this street, do not miss the house at numbers 48 and 50. This is the address of the **Baba Nonya Heritage Museum**, a treasure trove of exquisite Chinese furniture of mother-of-pearl and marble, silk embroidery, family heirlooms, lanterns, a bridal chamber complete with chamber pots and spittoon, beautiful silk painting and other elegant

WEST MALAYSIA

NEGERI SEMBILAN

MELAKA
Melaka

JOHOR

Straits of Malacca

BABAS AND NONYAS

When Sultan Mansur Shah married the Chinese princess Hang Lih Po she brought with her a 500-strong noble retinue from China. From their liaisons with the local Malays were born the Peranakan (which means 'born here') who are known as Babas (male) and Nonyas (female). In addition many Chinese merchants came to settle in the Straits and married Malay wives (hence the Peranakan are also known as 'Straits Chinese').

The Peranakan people represent the complete integration of Chinese immigrants with the native Malays. Examples of this unique melding extend from their language – Malay interlaced with Chinese – to their clothes: Nonyas wear *cheongsam* as well as *sarong kebaya*. Their epicurean skills blend Malay spices with southern Chinese cookery techniques, and have developed into one of Malaysia's most famous cuisines.

EXCURSIONS FROM MELAKA

Some 20km (12 miles) out-side Melaka is the Air Keroh Nature Belt along Air Keroh Road, which includes picnic areas, a nature park, and Mini Malaysia. This outdoor museum features traditional Malay houses from each of the thirteen states, with demonstrations of traditional pastimes and cultural shows. Nearby is the Melaka Zoo, voted the best among the southern states for its collection of wild and domestic animals kept in naturalistic surrroundings. There is a butterfly farm and a reptile farm where the trainers stage death-defying shows, wrestling with crocodiles and riding on their backs, as well as performing stunts like retrieving money from between their jaws.

paraphernalia. Girls dressed in sarongs and embroidered tops known as *kebaya* (the typical costume of the Nonyas) will take you on a guided tour round the grand mansion which belongs to the wealthy Chan family who made their fortune in the spice trade. Mr Chan Cheng Siew (of the second generation of the family) built the house in 1896. At the entrance, look out for the picture of the matriarch of the house, Mrs Chan, who was a larger-than-life lady in every sense of the word. Her massive, splendidly embroidered silk costume hangs on the wall as an exhibit. Today, the museum is looked after by Mr Chan Kim Lay, a member of the fourth generation, who is sometimes on hand to give a friendly talk about his fascinating family. This museum is more than an exhibition, it recreates the entire lifestyle of a typical wealthy Peranakan family during the early years of the 20th century. As part of the social elite of the time they entertained their colonial masters in the grand manner, as is evident from the display of expensive vintage brandy and whisky, silverware and fine porcelain dinner services. The museum opens from Saturday to Wednesday, 10:00 to 12:30 and 14:00 to 16:30, and on Thursday 09:00 to 12:00.

Jalan Hang Jebat, formerly known as Jonkers Street, is a haven for antique and bric-à-brac collectors. The rows of traditional shophouses are crammed with collectables dating as far back as the 17th century, in addition to modern souvenirs from Indonesia and other neigh-

The Cheng Hoon Teng Temple is Malaysia's oldest Chinese temple. Its name means 'Temple of the Evergreen Clouds'.

bouring countries. One could spend hours sifting through the artefacts and some shops even offer refreshing drinks of Chinese tea while you browse. Nearby at Jalan Tokong is the oldest temple in the country, **Cheng Hoon Teng Temple**, built in 1646 with materials imported from China. Mythological figures adorn the eaves of the roof while the interior of the temple is lavishly decorated with carvings and lacquerwork. The main altar is dedicated to the 'Goddess of Mercy' and a side altar is devoted to the 'Queen of Heaven', the guardian of fishermen and sailors.

Sam Po Kong Temple dates from 1795, and is dedicated to Admiral Cheng Ho, the eunuch envoy of the Chinese Ming Emperor, who first visited Melaka in 1409. It was said that during this journey, a bad storm tore a hole in his ship.

A Melakan trishaw driver takes a break. Trishaws offer a relaxing alternative to walking round the city.

Disaster would have struck had not a fish, known as Sam Po, plugged itself into the hole and saved the ship from sinking. The temple is located at the bottom of the massive hill of Bukit Cina ('Chinese Hill') which was the former residence of Princess Hang Lih Po and her 500 ladies-in-waiting when she arrived to marry Sultan Mansur Shah in 1459. Today it is the largest Chinese cemetery outside China and has 12,000 graves covering 25ha (62 acres) with many of the tombs dating back to the Ming period. The undulating terrain and peaceful location is also a favourite with joggers. Beside Sam Po Kong Temple is **Hang Lih Po's Well** (also known as the Sultan's Well) which was built for the princess. The well never dried up, even in times of drought. When the Dutch occupied Melaka, they built a strong wall round the well to ensure their exclusive use of it. It is said that those who drink the water are bound to return to Melaka but this theory cannot be put to the test as a metal grill now guards the well.

PULAU BESAR

For those who want to visit a beach resort whilst in Melaka, **Pulau Besar** (Big Island) is the place. It is an island 4km (2.5 miles) off the coast and is believed to be the site of one of the earliest civilizations of Malaysia. A small island, in spite of its name, it is one of the most beautiful along the Straits of Melaka with its lush tropical forest and tranquil emerald waters.

Beyond Kuala Lumpur at a Glance

Any time of year is good, though it can be quite rainy between May and Sep.

Genting Highlands: Bus services from KL (from Pudu Raya Bus Terminal) for which the fare includes the cable-car ride. There is also a taxi service from KL.

Fraser's Hill: Bus services from KL (at Pudu Raya Bus Terminal) to Kuala Kubu Bahru; connecting Fraser's Hill bus service operates twice daily at 08:00 and 12:00 uphill and 10:00 and 14:00 downhill. Taxis available from KL.

Cameron Highlands: By rail: KL to Tapah Road Station, about 2^1/$_2$hr; Tapah Road to Cameron Highlands 1^1/$_2$hr by taxi or bus. By road: from KL by taxi or bus takes 4hr.

Melaka and **Negeri Sembilan** are easily accessible via a very good highway from Kuala Lumpur and Singapore. There are frequent express bus services from Kuala Lumpur while taxis are readily available.

Malaysia Agriculture Park: accommodation in various styles from traditional farmers' homesteads to 'A-frame' huts and a campsite. Contact: Taman Pertanian Malaysia, Bukit Cahaya Sri Alam, 40000 Shah Alam, Selangor Darul Ehsan, tel (03) 5506922, fax (03) 550092.

Fraser's Hill
Luxury
Merlin Inn Resort, Jl. Lady Guilemard, tel (09) 382300: swimming pool.
Mid-range
Fraser's Hill Development Corp. Bungalows, Puncak Inn.

Cameron Highlands
Luxury
Strawberry Park, PO Box 81, tel (05) 901166, first-class hotel in beautiful hilltop setting, with modern facilities including swimming pool and a Chinese restaurant reputed to be the best in the Highlands. Popular with big groups of tourists and tends to be noisy when fully occupied;
Merlin Inn Resort, PO Box 4, Tanah Rata, Pahang 39007, tel (05) 491 1211, fax (05) 491 1178: overlooks golf course;
Ye Olde Smokehouse Country House Hotel, P O Box 77, Tanah Rata, Pahang 39007, tel (05) 491 1214: top of the range.
There are several inexpensive places to stay at Tanah Rata and Brinchang, from resthouses to moderately priced Chinese-operated hotels in shophouses:
Kowloon Hotel, 34-35 Jl

Besar, Brinchang, tel (05) 901366: has very good Chinese restaurant specializing in steamboat;
Parkland Hotel, 45 Jl Besar, tel (05) 901299 (two shops away from the Kowloon), owned by the same family, restaurant serves western cuisine. About ten minutes away, the Parkland Apartments offer one, two and three bedroom units.

Negeri Sembilan
Luxury
Allson Klana Resort, 4388 Jl Penghulu Cantik, Seremban, tel (06) 729600, fax (06) 739218;
Mid-range
Carlton Star Hotel, 47 Dato' Sheikh Ahmad, Seremban, tel (06) 736663, fax (06) 720040;
Tasik Hotel, Jl Tetamu, Seremban, tel (06) 730994, fax (06) 735355;
Ming Court Beach Hotel, Batu 7 1/2 Mile, Jl Pantai, Port Dickson, tel (06) 405244, fax (06) 405899;
Budget
Regency Hotel & Resort, Batu 5 1/2 Mile, Jl Pantai, Port Dickson, tel (06) 474090, fax (06) 475016;
Si-Rusa Inn, 7 Mile, Jl Pantai, Port Dickson, tel (06) 405233,

CAMERON HIGHLANDS	J	F	M	A	M	J	J	A	S	O	N	D
AVERAGE TEMP. °F	64	64	66	66	66	66	66	66	66	66	66	64
AVERAGE TEMP. °C	18	18	19	19	19	19	19	19	19	19	19	18
Hours of Sun Daily	5	5	5	5	5	5	4	4	4	4	3	3
RAINFALL in	5	4	8	11	11	5	7	9	9	13	12	8
RAINFALL mm	120	111	198	277	273	137	172	241	241	334	305	202
Days of Rainfall	10	11	14	16	13	9	10	11	13	17	18	15

fax (06) 405332.

Melaka
Luxury
Renaissance, Jl Bendahara, tel (06) 248888, fax 249269.
Mid-range
Emperor, Jl Munshi Abdullah, tel (06) 240777, fax 238989;
City Bayview, Jl Bendahara, tel (06) 239888, fax 236699;
Grand Continental Hotel, 20 Jl Tun Sri Lanang, tel (06) 240088, fax (06) 248125; and a wide selection of moderately priced accommodation

Pulau Besar
Tapa Nyai Island Resort, 37 Jl Chan Koon Cheng, tel (06) 456730, fax (06) 236739, built in typical kampung style, but with modern amenities including a swimming-pool.

WHERE TO EAT

Hill Resorts
Arzed Restoran, Puncak Inn, Fraser's Hill, tel (09) 382299;
Highlands Restaurant, 29 Jl Besar, Brinchang, Cameron Highlands, tel (09) 901309.
Negeri Sembilan
Blossom Court Chinese Restaurant, 2nd Floor, Allson Klana Resort, Seremban, tel (06) 729600;
Dragon Palace, Peninsula Plaza, Seremban, tel (06) 731385;
Restoran Sakura, 91-A Jl Tuanku Antah, Seremban, tel (06) 38933 (despite its Japanese name, it serves Cantonese and Malay food);
Syazan Café, 1 Kedai Mara,

Port Dickson, tel (06) 475885.

Melaka
Eating out in Melaka is an exciting experience. Nonya food features heavily in most restaurants.
Restoran Peranakan, Nam Hoe Villa at 317 Klebang Besar, tel 354436, a splendid mansion built at the turn of the century; its sister restaurant, **Restoran Peranakan Town House**, 107 Jl Tun Tan Cheng Lock, offers a cultural show nightly (except Saturdays);
Ole Sayang Restaurant, 198 & 199 Taman Melaka Jaya.
My Baba's, 164 Jl Munshi Abdullah.
Portuguese
Restoran de Lisbon, Portuguese Square;
Restoran de Portugis, San Pedro Restaurant, Portuguese Settlement;
Chinese
Hikeng, 112 Taman Melaka Jaya;
Lim Tian Puan, 251 Jl Tun Sri Lanang.
Stalls
Gluttons' Corner at Jl Taman, Bandar Hilir. The name says it all: here are numerous stalls selling various Chinese, Malay and Indian

dishes, from steamboat, satays and noodles to curries of all varieties.

TOURS AND EXCURSIONS

Light and sound tours of **Melaka** in the evening. Trips to **Pulau Besar**. Book with one of the following:
Annah (Melaka) Tours & Travel, 27 Jl Laksamana, tel (06) 235626;
MBTS Tour (Malacca), The City Bay View Hotel, Jl Bendahara, tel (06) 246251;
Melaka City Tours & Travel, Ground Floor, 11 Lorong Hang Jebat, tel (06) 244642;
Stadthuys Tours & Travel, Jl Bendahara, tel (06) 246373.

USEFUL CONTACTS

Genting Highlands: World Resort Berhad, 9th Floor, Wisma Genting, Jl Sultan Ismail, 50250 Kuala Lumpur, tel (03) 2613833/2622666, fax (03) 2616611;
Fraser's Hill Development Corporation, tel (09) 382044/382248;
Cameron Highlands Tourist Information Bureau, tel (05) 941266;
Malacca Tourist Information Centre, Jl Kota, tel (06) 236538, fax (06) 249686.

MELAKA	J	F	M	A	M	J	J	A	S	O	N	D
AVERAGE TEMP. °F	78	80	80	80	80	80	78	78	78	78	78	78
AVERAGE TEMP. °C	26	27	27	27	27	27	26	26	26	26	26	26
Hours of Sun Daily	6	7	7	7	7	6	7	6	6	6	5	5
RAINFALL in	3	4	6	8	7	7	7	7	8	8	9	5
RAINFALL mm	73	91	144	196	172	166	164	164	210	213	231	124
Days of Rainfall	7	7	10	13	12	10	12	12	18	17	17	11

4
The Northern States

The northern states of Perak, Penang (see p 75), Kedah and Perlis combine the natural beauty of rivers, lakes and mountains, with island resorts, historic sites and bustling border towns. The area is easily accessible from Penang or via the North-South Expressway from Kuala Lumpur or Thailand.

PERAK

Known as the 'Land of Grace', Perak covers an area of 21,000km² (8100 sq miles). Its name is probably derived from the Malay word *perak*, meaning 'silver', because of the silvery tin deposits found in abundance in the Larut area. The discovery of tin drew the attention of the outside world, bringing prosperity and, along with it, much turbulence. The Acehnese invaded in the 16th century, followed by the Dutch who built forts on Pulau Pangkor and at the mouth of the Perak River in the 17th century. In turn it was threatened by the Bugis in the south and the Thais in the north. The British came to its rescue in the 1820s but there were internal problems with the Malay sovereign while the Chinese immigrants squabbled over land rights and violent gang warfare broke out among the feuding factions. In 1896 Perak became one of the four Federated Malay States.

CLIMATE

• Taiping, in Perak, is claimed to be the wettest place in Malaysia, with an annual rainfall of more than 5000mm.
• The highest temperature ever recorded in Malaysia was 39.4°C (103°F) on Langkawi in March 1931.

Opposite: *A view from the north coast of the island of Langkawi, a tranquil paradise of soft sandy beaches and clear blue water.*

Ipoh **

Ipoh, with its grand colonial buildings, is the administrative and state capital. The first railway line in the Peninsula was laid here by the British to service the tin

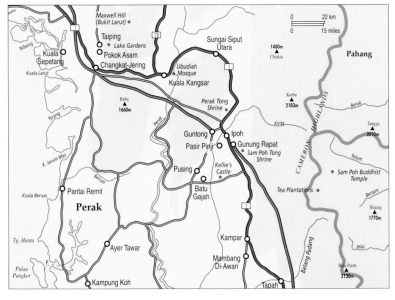

DON'T MISS

**Ipoh: Malaysia's best preserved Chinatown; spectacular cave temples.
*Kuala Kangsar: the royal town of Perak.
***Pulau Pangkor and Pulau Pangkor Laut: beautiful coral sand beaches.
***Langkawi: legendary islands, mountains and caves.

industry. Its railway station, with the adjoining Station Hotel, is similar in design to the one in Kuala Lumpur. South of Ipoh, about 5km (3 miles) away, is the cave temple of **Sam Poh Tong** in Gunung Rapat. It is reputed to be the biggest cave temple in Malaysia and dates from the 1890s. A monk passing through Ipoh from China found the cave and made it a place of meditation, occupying it himself for some twenty years. Buddhist monks and nuns still live there. Statues of the Buddha are interspersed among the stalactites and stalagmites. For the energetic, a steep climb of 246 steps will afford you a spectacular view of Ipoh and its surroundings. Outside the shrine is a Japanese garden with ponds containing carp and tortoises, symbols of longevity. There is a vegetarian restaurant in the grounds. Situated in the opposite direction, 6km (4 miles) north of Ipoh, is the **Perak Tong** temple in Gunung Tasek. Built in 1926, the temple has over 40 statues of Buddha including a seated Buddha that is 12.8m (42ft) high. A climb up 385 steps reveals a wonderful view of the Kinta Valley.

Taiping *

Travelling northwest along the Changkat-Jering Highway 55km (34 miles) from Ipoh is **Taiping**. Like Ipoh, it has its fair share of colonial buildings and edifices, especially along Jalan Taming Sari. The **Perak Museum**, built in 1887, is the oldest museum in Malaysia and has a very fine collection of aboriginal ornaments and archaeological treasures. The most notable landmark in Taiping is the **Lake Gardens**, converted in 1890 from old tin workings. Noted for being the wettest spot in Malaysia, this 64ha (160 acres) of garden is beautifully endowed with exuberant green turf and a profusion of trees and shrubs. There is a recreational park and a Japanese Garden in the grounds with Taiping Zoo, a 9-hole golf course and the colonial Taiping Rest House nearby.

Ipoh Railway Station, a Moorish edifice reminiscent of Kuala Lumpur's station building, dates from 1917. A small ipoh, or upas, tree, from which the city takes its name, is to be found in front of it.

Maxwell Hill

About 9km (6 miles) from Taiping is the oldest hill resort in Malaysia, **Bukit Larut**, more commonly known by its old colonial name of Maxwell Hill. Situated at an altitude of 1034m (3360ft), it is accessible only by four-wheel drive government Land Rovers which depart hourly from 08:00 to 18:00 daily for the journey up the steep winding road built by Japanese prisoners of war. At the summit on a clear day you can see Penang and Pulau Pangkor. It is a refreshing change to visit a hill resort without the modern trappings of the others: there is no commercial development here, just nature at its best.

Kuala Kangsar *

Halfway between Ipoh and Taiping is the royal town of Perak, where the sultan has his official residence at the Istana Iskandariah. Prior to the construction of this

---

A SCOTTISH CASTLE IN MALAYSIA

A bizarre landmark in Perak is **Kellie's Castle**, situated about 14km (9 miles) south of Ipoh on the road to Batu Gajah. It was begun in the late 19th century by a Scottish rubber tycoon, William Kellie Smith, and was designed in a fanciful Moorish style. Unfortunately he died of malaria before it was completed and the castle has since been neglected and allowed to fall into ruins. It stands eerily among the undergrowth on a hill in what was once his rubber estate. Overgrown with trees and bushes it resembles the castle of Sleeping Beauty.

The splendid Ubudiah Mosque in Kuala Kangsar, with its glittering golden domes, is one of Malaysia's most beautiful mosques.

palace in 1926, the royal family lived in the **Istana Kenangan**, in Jalan Istana, which is now the Museum di Raja. The old palace was built in traditional Malay style, apparently without any architectural plans and without using any nails. The other outstanding landmark in Kuala Kangsar is the **Ubudiah Mosque**, a fine example of Islamic architecture with its beautiful golden domes. The mosque was completed in 1917 after construction had twice been interrupted, first by the sultan's elephants when they accidentally trampled on the imported Italian tiles and second by the outbreak of World War I. South of the mosque is the 'Eton of the East', the exclusive **Malay College** built in 1905 for the children of the Malay élite.

Pulau Pangkor ★★

Lying off the coast of southern Perak, about 90km (56 miles) southwest of Ipoh, the island of Pangkor has many good beaches of golden sand lapped by clear waters. As this is the main island resort in the Straits of Melaka, it tends to get very crowded at weekends and during public and school holidays. The main beaches are concentrated on the western coastline. Among them are **Pantai Puteri Dewi** (Beach of the Lovely Princess), **Teluk Belanga** (Golden Sands) and **Pasir Bogak**, and there are a few more secluded bays at **Tortoise Bay**, **Teluk Nipah** and **Teluk Cempedak**.

The old ruins of the Dutch Fort at Teluk Gedung are a reminder of the colonial past when the Dutch attempted to control the tin trade in the 17th century. The picturesque fishing villages with their quaint coffee shops add colour to the very easygoing island lifestyle.

THE LEANING TOWER OF TELUK INTAN

While the Leaning Tower of Pisa is internationally well-known, the leaning clock-tower of Teluk Intan is virtually unheard of. Yet it is the second largest tower so inclined. It was built in 1885 by a Chinese tin baron, Leong Choon Chong, in the style of a Chinese pagoda. It stood at an imposing height of 25.5m (84ft) but it started to tilt slowly between 1889 and 1895 owing to its unstable foundations. The local inhabitants believed that the tower was under a curse and some even moved away. Teluk Intan is in southern Perak on the Perak River, 90km (56 miles) from Ipoh.

Pulau Pangkor Laut ★★★

This 120ha (300 acre) island lying off the southwest tip of Pulau Pangkor is privately owned and run as the Pangkor Laut Resort. Too small to attract any permanent settlement, it was once a pirate's hideaway, but is now the most exclusive island resort in Malaysia. It is concentrated on **Royal Bay**, but the sea here is disappointingly muddy and there are many sea urchins amongst the rocks. On the other side of the island, accessible by a path through the jungle or by boat, is **Emerald Bay**. In contrast to Royal Bay, here a beautiful white sandy beach sweeps round the secluded cove and the water, which is indeed emerald green, is invitingly clear and warm and ideal for scuba diving and snorkelling. Emerald Bay has been voted one of the best 100 beaches of the world. **Marina Bay**, accessible along a path from Emerald Bay, is another delightful cove, with a clean beach and clear blue sea. As this is a private island, no day trippers are permitted in the resort.

WEST MALAYSIA

PERAK

Pangkor

Pangkor
Laut

Straits of Malacca

KEDAH

Documented by Chinese pilgrims in the seventh century and Arab traders in the ninth century, Kedah is Malaysia's oldest state, though its early importance as a trading post declined as Melaka rose to prominence on the trade route between India and China. Today, with Perlis, the state is Malaysia's main producer of rice. Its other primary industries are fishing and tourism. The influence of its proximity to Thailand can be seen in both its architecture and its cuisine.

Alor Setar ★

The state capital boasts some interesting historical buildings, including the **Zahir Mosque**, completed in 1912, with its distinctive black domes. The nearby **Balai Nobat**, a pagoda-like structure built in 1907, houses the ancient royal orchestra. The **Balai Besar** or Great Hall is a fine example of Malay-Thai architecture built in 1898, and is the official venue for the sultan's audiences on his birthday and other special occasions. The elegant **State**

F. SPENCER CHAPMAN

During World War II, a British commando, F. Spencer Chapman, DSO, escaped from the mainland in a sampan, reaching Pankor Laut after 15 perilous days at sea. After spending three-and-a-half harrowing years in the Malayan jungle fighting the Japanese, his final objective was to get to Pangkor Laut to wait for a submarine pick-up before the British launched a major offensive against the invading Imperial army. On 13 May 1944, he and his compatriot, Major R. Broome, made their final escape from Emerald Bay on the island and were picked up by the submarine, *The Statesman*, on which they endured another seven dangerous days' journey to Ceylon (Sri Lanka). Spencer Chapman later wrote a book, *The Jungle Is Neutral* (1949) recounting his experiences as a guerrilla fighter in Malaya and he devoted a chapter to the submarine pick-up at Emerald Bay.

Candi Bukit Batu Pahat, 'Temple of the Hill of Chiselled Stone', the most important Hindu temple unearthed so far in the excavations in the Bujang Valley.

Museum is again in classic Malay-Thai style and its exhibits include some of the finds from the Bujang Valley.

Gunung Jerai ★

This massive limestone outcrop standing at 1200m (3937ft) has been a landmark for sailors over the centuries. It is now a recreational park with scenic walks and waterfalls. There is a forestry museum at the peak.

LANGKAWI

Situated 30km (19 miles) off the coast of Perlis is a cluster of 105 islands collectively known as Langkawi (although the name really belongs to the biggest and only fully inhabited island in the group). Tourism came to Langkawi late in 1987 when it was declared a duty free port. Despite its recent rise to fame in the forefront of tourism, the island has managed to retain its rural charm, with quaint Malay villages, *padi* fields and rubber plantations. The natives seem to take the onslaught of tourism in their stride.

The islands, mountains and caves of Langkawi are shrouded in mystery and legends. The island is dominated by three mountains, Gunung Macincang and Gunung Raya, with the smaller Gunung Sawar wedged between them. Legend has it that these mountains were once two feuding men, Mat Chincang and Mat Raya. Their son and daughter, however, fell in love, despite their families' disapproval. Matters came to a head on the wedding day and the two fathers started a fight. Soon the celebration became a fiasco, as pots and pans were used as missiles. A pot of curry crashed to the ground on the site of the village now called **Kampung Belanga Pecah** ('Broken Cooking Pot Village'). The gravy began to seep into the ground in the area today called **Kisap** ('seep in').

> **BUJANG VALLEY**
>
> Nestled between Gunung Jerai and Sungai Muda, this is one of the richest archaeological sites in Malaysia, where evidence has been found of an early Hindu civilization dating back to the seventh century. A total of 50 *candi* (temples) have been discovered, indicating the original grandeur of the place. Many of the finds are now displayed at the Bujang Valley Archaeological Museum in Pengkalan Bujang.

The spot where the gravy stopped its flow is now **Kuah** ('gravy'), the capital of Langkawi. In the ensuing battle, a huge cauldron of hot water was flung and split over the area of **Telaga Air Hangat** ('hot water') where there are three hot springs. Mat Sawar, a mutual friend of the two families, eventually stopped the fighting. The two perpetrators repented, and in remorse, they were transformed into mountains. Mat Sawar still stands guard between them.

Kuah Town *

Before the advent of tourism in Langkawi, Kuah was a sleepy little village servicing the needs of rubber tappers, farmers and fishermen. The wooden shophouses along the only street were run by the small Chinese population and offered a limited selection of goods. Today Kuah has rather more than one street and boasts duty free shops, restaurants and hotels. A new centre at Jalan Air Hangat has been built to cater for this rapid growth. Apart from shopping, there is little to do in the town itself.

Mahsuri's Mausoleum **

From Kuah town, head west on Jalan Padang Matsirat to the white marble tomb of Mahsuri. A typical Malay house stands by the well she used, with kapok trees and a large aviary of white doves which were her favourite pets. In the village square, a giant sculpture of a *kris* marks the spot where Mahsuri was executed. Nearby is the cultural centre of **Tanamas** with a traditional Malay show-house, pottery and batik demonstrations and a souvenir shop. A small orchestra plays traditional Malay music, but is drowned out occasionally by the loud racket of pop music playing in the same compound. The centre is open from 08:30 to 18:00.

THE CURSE OF MAHSURI
The beautiful Mahsuri caught the eye of the local chieftain who desired her to become his second wife. To prevent this, the chieftain's jealous wife match-made her to their son, and subsequently accused her of adultery. Despite her protest of innocence and the lack of any evidence, Mahsuri was sentenced to death and was executed in the village square. With her dying breath she laid a curse on Langkawi, proclaiming that the island would enjoy neither prosperity nor peace for seven generations. Soon after her death, Langkawi was invaded by the Thais and there followed years of droughts and floods causing bad harvests. Now, after seven generations, prosperity and peace are restored at last with the wealth and employment tourism is generating in the islands.

The Field of Burnt Rice *

Beras Terbakar, 'the Field of Burnt Rice', is at Kampung Raja in the district of Padang Matsirat. Soon after Mahsuri's death, Langkawi was attacked by the Thais. The chieftain, her erstwhile father-in-law, ordered the rice stock of the island to be buried to prevent the marauding Thai army from laying their hands on it. The villagers set fire to the granary to fool their enemies into thinking that the entire stock had been burnt. Unfortunately the heat from the fire permeated the ground and charred the rice. On rainy days, some of the burnt rice grains are still being washed up to the surface.

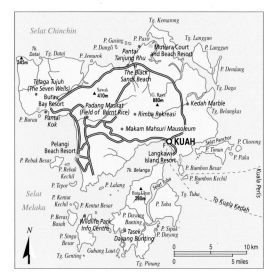

Gunung Raya ★★

A detour into the district of Ulu Melaka leads to a very good road up the legendary Gunung Raya with scenic views of the coasts below. The meandering road climbs gently along the back of the range and up a steep path leading to a tea-house. A high wooden tower now provides only a partial view of Langkawi, through tall trees (in keeping with the local policy of ecotourism, no trees may be cut down unnecessarily).

Pantai Cenang ★★★

Travelling southwest down the coast, a left turn on the main road from the airport will take you to one of the most famous beaches on the island (albeit not the best). The white sand stretches on for miles, dotted with accommodation of all types from modestly priced huts and motels to the deluxe **Pelangi Beach Resort**, designed and built like a traditional Malay village for the Commonwealth leaders attending the Commonwealth Heads of Government Meeting in October 1989. Since then it has been a harbinger for this type of architecture in other resorts in Langkawi.

Water buffaloes roam freely on Langkawi.

Pantai Kok ★★

This is the budget traveller's paradise with an abundance of good value-for-money thatched huts and chalets on a beautiful beach. It has a informal, laid-back atmosphere and the dollars stretch further here. If you can tear yourself away from the lovely beach, trek into the jungle nearby in search of adventure amongst the dense growth and cool down at **Telaga Tujuh** ('The Seven Wells'). A

Pantai Pasir Hitam, or Black Sand Beach, on the island of Langkawi. The sand is not really black but streaked with mineral deposits.

series of cascading waterfalls drop from a height of 90m (300ft) into seven deep pools.

Teluk Datai **

At Pantai Kok, the road veers inland northwards and if you follow Jalan Datai going northwest it will take you to one of the most spectacular sights in Langkawi, Teluk Datai. The winding road is flanked on one side by a sheer drop to the azure sea, and on the other by the lush greenery cloaking the wall-like flanks of Gunung Macincang. The road ends at the new deluxe resort of **The Datai**, where the beach is one of the best on the island – the pure white sand is lapped gently by the calm Andaman Sea, and Thailand is just a glimpse away.

Pantai Pasir Hitam *

To explore the northern part of the island, travel back down Jalan Datai to the junction, then turn left travelling northeastward towards **Pantai Pasir Hitam** ('Black Sand Beach') passing the crocodile farm, where a thousand of these reptiles are reared for their skin and to amuse visitors by wrestling with their trainers.

BUFFALOES

Buffaloes used for ploughing fields on Langkawi are also a symbol of wealth among the Malays and these beasts of burden are said to outnumber by far the Chinese and Indian populations of this predominantly Malay island. (If you are driving on the island at night, be warned that these beasts have right of way and have no respect for the highway code. They have been known to cause serious road accidents.)

The blue waters of Pregnant Maiden Lake on Pulau Dayang Bunting.

Pantai Tanjung Rhu ***

This beach, whose name means 'the Cape of Pine Trees', is surprisingly undeveloped and under-used, since it is the finest stretch of pristine beach on Langkawi. There are a few stalls selling souvenirs, drinks and snacks. There are no chalets or huts on the beach but set slightly inland is the **Mutiara Court and Beach Resort**, the only resort on this part of the island. Its concrete structure is a blot on the hitherto serene landscape. This cape is an ideal place for a day away from the crowds.

Island Hopping

From the jetty in Kuah you can take bunk-boats which leave hourly for **Pulau Dayang Bunting**, the second largest island in the group, and **Pulau Singa Besar** ('Island of the Big Lion') which has a wildlife park where mouse-deer, iguanas, monkeys and exotic birds (who fly free on the island) can be found. There is a wide choice of islands to visit and most of them have beautiful sandy coves and clear waters with rich marine life for scuba diving and snorkelling. Boats can also be hired from Pantai Cenang.

Pulau Bayar *

For diving enthusiasts, the **Pulau Bayar Marine Park** is worth a visit. It comprises four small coral islands, 13km (18 miles) west of Kuala Kedah and 3 hours' journey from Langkawi. The crystal clear water abounds with coral gardens and fish of all colours and sizes. There is no accommodation on the islands but there are picnic tables and washing facilities. Permits have to be obtained from the Fisheries Department in Alor Setar or Kuala Lumpur if you wish to set up camp.

PERLIS

Nestled against the Thai border, this is the smallest and most northerly state of Malaysia and is known as the 'Rice Bowl' of the country. Its economy is mainly agrarian, with rice, rubber and sugar as the main crops in addition to fruit. Its rural scenery, with its rolling carpets of green *padi* fields, remains unspoilt.

Kangar *

The state capital is a rustic little town surrounded by *padi* fields and trading mostly in seafood and agricultural produce. The main places of interest are the **State Mosque** and the **Dato Wan Ahmad house** of traditional wooden construction with ornate carvings.

Arau, the royal town of Perlis, is 10km (6 miles) from Kangar. Fruit trees line the avenues running between quaint traditional houses. The **Royal Palace** fronts the main road with the **Royal Mosque** nearby.

Gua Kelam Kaki Bukit *

This is a limestone cave, literally the 'Cave of Darkness at the Foothill', in the small town of Kaki Bukit, 26km (16 miles) from Kangar. It is about 370m (1214ft) long and has a working tin mine which is accessed by a suspension bridge over a subterranean stream.

Padang Besar *

On the border between Malaysia and Thailand, this bustling town's main attraction is as a hunting-ground for bargains. Its numerous shops and stalls sell goods from both sides of the border. Here the two countries merge into one and the only signs of a national border are the Immigration and Customs counters.

> **A CHEQUERED HISTORY**
>
> Perlis was for many years a pawn in the political arena. It was once part of Kedah, which was conquered by the Thais in 1821, but when Kedah was restored to the sultan Perlis remained in Thai hands as a separate state until it was transferred to British rule by the Anglo-Thai treaty of 1909. During World War II the occupying Japanese handed it back to Thailand, but after the surrender of the Imperial Army it came under British protection once again until it joined the Federation of Malaya in 1957.

A dramatic limestone outcrop towers above the padi *fields of Perlis, the 'Rice Bowl' of Malaysia.*

The Northern States at a Glance

This is an all-year-round destination as there is no distinct rainy season, although rain is more frequent between May and Sep, and very little rain falls during Jan and Feb.

Northern Malaysia is easily accessible by rail, road, air and sea from various gateway points. From the south, railway lines and roads run from Singapore up the west coast to the northern states and from the north from Thailand. There are seaports at Langkawi, Penang, Lumut in Perak and Kuala Kedah in Kedah, including a ferry link to Medan in Indonesia. There are international airports at Penang and Langkawi and domestic airports at Ipoh and Alor Setar.

Maxwell Hill: Accessible only in Government Land Rovers which leave Taiping (just above the Lake Gardens) every hour from 08:00 to 18:00.

Pangkor: Accessible by air from Kuala Lumpur (50 minutes), Penang (35 minutes) and Singapore (95 minutes) with Pelangi Air. The sea journey is from Lumut, the ferry terminal, 288km (180 miles) from Kuala Lumpur, 180km (112 miles) from Penang and 83km (52 miles) from Ipoh.

Pulau Pangkor Laut: The island can be reached by ferry from Lumut or Pangkor.

Langkawi has daily flights from Kuala Lumpur, Penang and Singapore. There are ferry services from Kuala Perlis (45mins) and from Kuala Kedah (one hour) to Kuah.

There are car rental firms in Penang, Langkawi, Ipoh and Alor Setar. Taxis are available in most major towns; interstate taxis have a fixed price. Trishaws are a novel way of getting about in Kangar and Alor Setar: negotiate the fare before boarding. Buses are an economical way of travelling from town to town.

The best way to get around on Langkawi is to hire motorcycles or cars which are readily available for hire from most of the island's resorts and Kuah town.

Ipoh
Luxury
Excelsior Hotel, 43 Clarke Street, tel (05) 536666, fax (06) 536912;
The Syuen Hotel, 88 Jl Sultan Abdul Jalil, tel (05) 538889, fax (05) 533335.
Mid-range
Tambun Inn, Tambun Road, tel (05) 577211, fax (05) 567887;
Ritz Garden, 79 Jl C M Yusuff, tel (05) 547777, fax (05) 545222.
Budget
Wan Wah Hotel, 32-38 Jl Ali Pitchay, tel (06) 515177;
Caspian Hotel, 6-8-10 Jl Jubilee, tel (06) 542324.

Taiping
Mid-range
Panorama Hotel, 61-79 Jl Kota, tel (05) 834111, fax (05) 834129;
Cempaka Sari, 1 Jl Sultan Mansor Shah, tel (05) 822044;
Furama Hotel, 30 Jl Peng Loong, tel (05) 821077, fax (05) 825294.
Budget
Cheong Onn Hotel, 24B Jl Iskandar, tel (05) 821815;
Happiness Air-Condition Hotel, 28 Jl Simpang, tel (05) 821933;
Malaya Hotel, 52 Market Square, tel (05) 823733.

Langkawi
Luxury
The Datai, Jl Teluk Datai, tel (04) 955 2500, fax (04) 955 2600, rustically styled individual villas; beautiful 18-hole championship golf course;
Pelangi Beach Resort, Jl Pantai Cenang, tel (04) 955 1001, fax (04) 955 1122;
Berjaya Langkawi Beach Resort, P O Box 200, Teluk Burau, tel (04) 959 1888, fax (04) 959 1886;
Sheraton Langkawi Resort, Teluk Nibong, tel (04) 955 1901, fax (04) 955 1968;
Burau Bay Resort, Teluk Burau, tel (04) 955 1062, fax (04) 955 1172, individual cabanas in beautiful garden;
Langkawi Holiday Villa, Lot 1698, Pantau Tengah, tel (04) 955 1701, fax (04) 955 1504.
Mid-range
Delima Resort, Pantai

The Northern States at a Glance

Tengah, tel (04) 955 1801, fax (04) 955 1811, largest resort on island with 1500 rooms;
Langkawi Island Resort, Jl Pantai Dato' Syed Omar, tel (04) 966 6209, fax (04) 966 6414;
Radissons Langkawi, Tanjung Rhu, tel (04) 959 1091, fax (04) 959 1211.
Budget
Cenang Beach Resort, Pantai Cenang, tel (04) 911395;
Country Beach Hotel, Pantai Kok, tel (04) 911212, fax (04) 911066;
Coral Beach Motel, Jl Pantai Kok, tel (04) 955 1000.

Maxwell Hill
Visitors can either stay at **Larut Rest House** or in bungalows at the top of the hill. Contact the Superintendent, Maxwell Hill, Taiping, tel (05) 827241.

Pulau Pangkor
Accommodation ranges from the luxury **Pan Pacific Resort** at Teluk Belanga, with its elegantly appointed rooms, to smaller moderately priced hotels, 'A-frame' huts and government rest houses.
Pangkor Laut Resort, tel (05) 685 1375, fax (05) 685 1320.

WHERE TO EAT

Hawkers' stalls and coffee shops everywhere offer inexpensive local cuisine.

Ipoh
Hong Kong Oil Chicken and Roast Duck, 638 Jl Kuala Kangsar, tel (05) 564550;
King Pan Seafood Restaurant, 26 Jl Leong Sin Nam, tel (05) 530409;
Perwira Restoran, 154 Jl Gopeng, tel (05) 202750.

Taiping
Kentucky Restaurant, 25 Jl Kota, tel (05) 825012.

Langkawi
There are many eating places in Kuah while all the resorts have their own restaurants. At Air Hangat village you can sample traditional Malay food while watching a cultural performance.
Barn Thai 'jazzaurant', Kampung Belanga Pecah, Kisap, tel (04) 966 6699. Authentic Thai food, much celebrated and more expensive than restaurants in Kuah. Shuttle service from leading hotels and resorts;
Bon Ton at the Beach, Pantai Cenang, tel (04) 912355;
Hoover Restoran, 51 Dingdong, Kuah, tel (04) 788805;
Restaurant Sari Seafood, Pusat Pelancongan Langkawi, Komplex Market Lama, Kuah, tel (04) 917193;
Restoran Everybody, 102 Taman Medan Berjaya, Kuah, tel (04) 916213.

TOURS AND EXCURSIONS

Langkawi
Organized tours round Langkawi and neighbouring islands, boat trips and fishing trips can be booked through main hotels.
Pulau Bayar: Some tour companies in Kuala Lumpur and Penang operate tours to Pulau Bayar [eg Asian Overland Services, tel (03) 2925622] and Pernas OUE Cruises operate cruises from Penang Mutiara Beach Resort or Pelangi Beach Resort at Langkawi.

USEFUL CONTACTS

Malaysia Tourism Promotion Board (Northern Region), 10 Jl Tun Syed Sheh Barakbah, 10200 Pulau Pinang, tel (04) 620066/619067, fax (04) 623688;
Perak Tourist Information Centre, State Economic Planning Unit, Jl Dato' Sago, 3000 Ipoh, tel (05) 532800/531957.

LANGKAWI	J	F	M	A	M	J	J	A	S	O	N	D
AVERAGE TEMP. °F	82	84	84	86	84	82	82	82	80	80	82	82
AVERAGE TEMP. °C	28	29	29	30	29	28	28	28	27	27	28	28
Hours of Sun Daily	8	8	8	7	6	4	5	5	5	5	6	8
RAINFALL in	1	1	2	5	12	10	11	11	16	12	7	2
RAINFALL mm	30	21	49	121	319	259	291	272	399	309	176	59
Days of Rainfall	4	3	5	10	21	19	19	19	23	22	16	8

5
Penang

Penang, known as 'the Pearl of the Orient', lies off the northwest coast of Peninsular Malaysia. It was originally settled by Ragam, an early trader from Sumatra. He called the island 'Pulau Bersatu' which means 'Single Island'. It is said that the present airport on Penang which is called Bayan Lepas ('free parakeet') is built on the site where Ragam set free some parakeets. Later, the Portuguese, in their search for new colonies and spices, discovered the island and called it 'Pulo Pinaom' after the betel nut palms (*pinang* in Malay) which grew in abundance there.

In 1771, **Captain Francis Light** of the British East India Company set sail to Sumatra and the Malay Peninsula looking for a suitable trading post. After some negotiation with the sultan of Kedah who ruled Penang at that time, the East India Company set up a naval base on the island in 1786. Francis Light promptly hoisted the British flag in the name of King George III and renamed the island after the Prince of Wales. This infuriated the sultan as Light had pre-empted any formal treaty, and he attempted to repel the British. But his army of 10,000 men was no match for Captain Light's forces who were better equipped. The sultan reluctantly retreated and settled for a treaty in 1791. In return for occupying the island, the British agreed to pay an annual sum of 6,000 Spanish dollars, the recognized currency at that time, to the sultan. This promise is still kept today by the state government of Penang, which makes a token annual contribution of RM10,000 to the Sultan of Kedah.

CLIMATE

Penang's sunniest weather comes in June and July, and from December to April. Its rainy season is in September and October, but it gets very little rainfall in January and February as it is shielded from the effects of the northeast monsoon.

Opposite: *The distinctive red roofscape of Georgetown, the capital of Penang, its narrow streets bordered by rows of shophouses and covered 'five-foot ways'.*

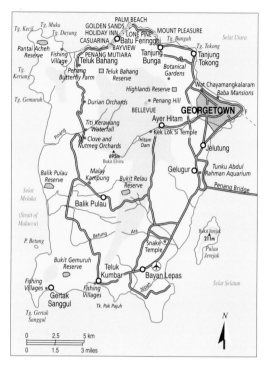

When the British occupied the island, it had a population of only about 1000, mainly Malay fishermen. It is said that as an enticement to the men to clear the jungle for him, Francis Light fired Spanish silver dollars into the undergrowth from a cannon. Soon the trees were cleared and tracks were carved out of the forest while shelters were built together with a wooden stockade. Light declared the island a free port and offered further encouragement to traders by giving generous land grants. Immigrants, particularly the Chinese, flocked to settle on the island and the area began to prosper.

Within a short time, Penang was flourishing as a busy port with its natural harbour. For a short time it became the capital of the Straits Settlements: the British territories of Melaka, Singapore and Penang itself, until it was eclipsed by the greater glory of Singapore. Penang enjoyed further periods of prosperity during the 1850s with the discovery of tin deposits on the mainland nearby, and at the peak of the rubber industry in the early 20th century. Some of the opulent mansions built during these boom times are still to be seen dotted about the island.

In 1800, an area on the mainland called Province Wellesley was added and is today linked by a bridge to the island. On 31 August 1957 Penang became a state in the Federation of Malaya when Britain relinquished its rule and Malaya became an independent country.

DON'T MISS

** Georgetown's historic centre: Fort Cornwallis and Penang Museum
*** Khoo Kongsi: The lavish Chinese Dragon Mountain Hall.
** Penang Hill: Funicular railway to spectacular views.
*** Kek Lok Si Temple: The most beautiful Buddhist temple in Southeast Asia.
*** Penang's beaches: World famous Batu Feringghi.

GEORGETOWN

The chequered history of Penang is today reflected in its variety of cultures and traditions, its narrow streets of old shophouses, its grand mansions, especially along Jalan Sultan Ahmad Shah ('Millionaires' Row') and the handsome colonial edifices of Georgetown, its capital. The old town is a maze of narrow streets, and is small enough for it to be most enjoyably explored on foot. Many streets have covered 'five-foot ways' in front of the shophouses to shelter pedestrians from both sun and rain, and these make for cooler walking. Hiring a trishaw is a good alternative.

Fort Cornwallis *

The fortress built on the spot where Francis Light first landed in Penang in 1786 today still stands guard on the seafront, complete with cannons. Originally built in wood, it was replaced by a stone construction using convict labour in 1804-5. It never had any military importance and the cannons were never fired in defence. The compound within the fort is now converted into a park with souvenir shops, stalls and an amphitheatre used for concerts and shows. There is a model of a typical Malay house near the souvenir shops. Shoes must be removed before entering the house.

The Jubilee Clocktower was erected in 1897 at the expense of a Chinese millionaire to celebrate Queen Victoria's Diamond Jubilee year. The tower is 60ft (18m) high – a foot for each year of her reign.

THE LEGEND OF SRI RAMBAI

The **Sri Rambai** is a brass cannon of fine craftsmanship, presented by the Dutch to the sultan of Johor in 1606. In 1616, it was captured by the Achenese and remained in Aceh until 1795, when it was sent as a gift to the sultan of Selangor. In 1871 it was captured by the British amongst other spoils and taken to Penang aboard the steamer *Sri Rambai*, after which it came to be named. Sri Rambai is today revered as a living entity with mystical powers. According to local belief, barren women may be blessed with children if they lay flowers on its barrel and offer special prayers.

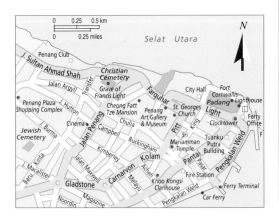

The 65-storey Komtar, housing offices, shops, an auditorium, cinema and restaurants, towers over the old houses on stilts that line the bustling waterfront.

Penang Museum and Art Gallery **

Within walking distance of the fort, in Lebuh Farquhar, this museum traces the history of Penang and includes an exhibition of the Peranakan heritage. In front of the museum is the statue of Francis Light modelled after his son William, the founder of Adelaide in South Australia, as there was no known portrait of the man himself. The museum is open from 09:00 to 17:00 daily except on Friday when it is closed between 12:15 and 14:45 for Friday prayers. Nearby is the Anglican **St George's Church**. An elegant example of Georgian architecture, it was built in 1818. In the churchyard is the simple tomb of Francis Light who died in 1794 of malaria, only eight years after founding the colony.

Cheong Fatt Tze Mansion **

This magnificent house in Lebuh Leith was built in the 1880s by Thio Thiaw Siat, a Kwantung businessman, using a team of skilled Chinese craftsmen. It is believed to be one of only three such buildings outside China. Surrounded by a 3m (10ft) wall, it has sumptuously decorated ceremonial halls, bedrooms and libraries linked by a maze of small gardens and cobbled stone courtyards. The grand spiral staircase, stained glass windows, lattice screens, silk scrolls, tapestries and an Aladdin's cave of sculptures, porcelain, carvings, lacquers, bronze and furniture all add to its charm and beauty.

Georgetown's Temples **

The diversity of religious belief in Penang is reflected in the number of places of worship crowded into the same vicinity. **Kapitan Kling Mosque**, in the street which now

---

THE EASTERN AND ORIENTAL HOTEL

Opened more than a century ago by Martin and Tigram Sarkies, the Armenian brothers who also established the famous Raffles Hotel in Singapore and the Strand in Rangoon, this grand old hotel still maintains its atmosphere of colonial elegance. Affectionately known as the 'E & O', in its heyday before World War II it entertained such luminaries as Somerset Maugham, Noel Coward and Hermann Hesse, while the actress Rita Hayworth sunbathed on the hotel's seafront terrace.

Blue dragons and exuberant flower arrangements proliferate on the massive roof of the Khoo Kongsi, the most splendid of Penang's Chinese clan houses.

bears its name, was built by Muslims from southern India, or Kling, in the early 19th century. On the same road is the **Temple of the Goddess of Mercy**, the oldest temple in Penang, built in 1800. Nearby is the Indian Temple of **Sri Mariamman**, built in 1883 and ornately decorated with figures from the Hindu pantheon. The statue of Lord Subramaniam, which is used to lead the procession to the Waterfall Temple during Thaipusam (see page 26), is dripping with jewels.

Khoo Kongsi ★★★

The Khoo clan originally came from the Hokkien Province in China. Their magnificent clan house at Cannon Square is lavishly decorated, with an especially ornate roof sporting blue dragons intertwined among mythological figures, flowers and birds. All this paraphernalia reputedly weighs 25 tons. Inside, walls, pillars and windows are exquisitely carved with figures depicting Chinese legends including a series of stories of filial piety, since love and respect for parents and elders are of paramount importance in Chinese society. Across the square is a Chinese opera theatre. Permission to visit the temple has to be obtained from the Khoo clan office situated on the right hand side of the temple. Opening hours are from 09:00 to 17:00 Mondays to Fridays and 09:00 to 13:00 on Saturdays.

THE CHINESE CLAN HOUSE

The aim of the clan house is to look after the welfare of clan members, assisting new arrivals in the country and safeguarding the shrines of the clan's ancestors.

In 1894, the wealthy Khoo clan built a new temple in place of the original building of 1850 for the worship of their patron saint, Tua Sai Yeah, a general of the Ch'in Dynasty in the 3rd century BC. The new building was a very ambitious and expensive project, fashioned after a grand Chinese palace, and took eight years to finish. Soon after completion, the temple was burnt down by a mysterious fire. It was said that the building was too noble for the saint and for the memorial tablets of ordinary mortals. It was believed that its extravagance and opulence had offended the gods. The temple was rebuilt on a more modest scale, though with the finest materials meticulously crafted by highly skilled artisans from China.

*Malaysia's only funicular
railway copes with the
steep gradient of Penang
Hill.*

AROUND THE ISLAND

To get a spectacular panoramic view of Penang, take the
funicular railway from Ayer Hitam station to **Penang
Hill**, 830m (2700ft) above sea level. The pleasant journey
takes 30 minutes with a change of train midway. Along
the way, orchids, pitcher plants, durian trees and other
tropical vegetation grow along the embankment,
enlivened by the ubiquitous macaques sitting by the railway track or leaping about the trees. Further up the hill,
grand mansions with red roof tiles perch on the hillside
amongst beautifully manicured gardens. At journey's
end, there is a kiosk selling food and drinks, and a van-
tage point from which you can gaze out over
Georgetown, the red tiled roofs of the shophouses looking like a patchwork quilt. There is also a hawkers' centre further up towards the summit, where an Indian temple and a mosque sit side by side. For those who want to
stay overnight, the Bellevue Hotel provides comfortable
accommodation. This old hotel has a bird park by its
entrance with a small collection of exotic birds including
some very noisy macaws. A path leads down to the
Botanical Garden which has 30ha (75 acres) of tropical
plants. Look out for the Cannon Ball trees near the
entrance with the brown fruits from which they get their
name clustering around their trunks. Here too is the
home of the macaques who roam freely and rob visitors
of their food and drinks (so watch out!).

Kek Lok Si Temple ***

The largest, and arguably the most beautiful, Buddhist
temple in Southeast Asia stands majestically on a hill at
Ayer Hitam, a small town in the centre of the island. The
temple sprawls over a wide area with praying halls dedicated to various gods, interspersed with pagodas with
numerous statues of the Buddha in many manifestations.
The most outstanding feature is the seven-storey pagoda
which forms the focal point of the complex. Standing at
30m (98ft) tall, the tower was constructed in three different architectural styles. The octagonal base is typically
Chinese, the middle tiers are Thai, and the whole edifice

is topped with a golden Burmese spiral dome. Each tier has an altar dedicated to the Buddha and the Goddess of Mercy. It is customary to make a small donation (the amount at your discretion) to gain access to the top of the pagoda, which affords a spectacular view of Ayer Hitam.

Wat Chayamangkalaram Thai Temple **

This gaudily painted Thai Buddhist temple at Lorong Burmah is guarded by two fearsome-looking gods while giant multi-headed dragons flank the way to the entrance. This temple houses the world's third largest reclining Buddha, measuring 33m (108ft). On the left hand side of the main altar is the figure of a monk in a lotus position. It is believed that this is the actual pre-served body of the founder of the temple. Thin sheets of gold leaf cover his face and limbs. Behind the giant Buddha is a crypt where the ancestral ashes of families of devotees who donated money to the temple are kept in niches on the walls with tablets bearing the names and pictures of the deceased. Across the road is the **Burmese temple**, on a smaller scale but equally beautiful, with a colourful altar of red and gold and a seated giant Buddha in the centre. Saffron-robed monks are on hand

The seven-storey pagoda of the vast Kek Lok Si Temple, built in a variety of styles by Chinese, Thai and Burmese craftsmen.

Holiday-makers on the renowned Feringghi Beach, 3km (2 miles) of white sand along Penang's north coast.

to bless and counsel the faithful about their everyday problems.

The Snake Temple *

Further south, on the road to the airport, the Temple of the Azure Cloud was built in 1850 in memory of a Buddhist priest Chor Soo Kong, who was believed to possess spiritual healing powers. Here in the incense-smoke-filled temple are green and black striped pit vipers coiled round twigs placed on the altars. Most of these poisonous snakes have been rendered harmless by having their fangs removed. The incense seems to have a sedative effect on them as they are completely oblivious to the tourists who coil them round their neck for pictures taken by officially appointed photographers. The proceeds from the photographs go towards the upkeep of the temple. The number of snakes has dwindled over the years although it seems mysteriously to increase at the time of the monk's birthday in July. The snakes are believed to be the incarnation of the monk.

Penang's Beach Resorts

No journey to Penang is complete without time to enjoy the famous sandy beaches which stretch from **Tanjung Bungah** through the main coastal thoroughfare of **Batu Feringghi** (Foreigner's Rock) to the fishing village of **Teluk Bahang**. Whilst most of the beaches have beautiful clean sand, they do not have the advantage of the clear waters of the East Coast and those near the city suffer from pollution. Accommodation to suit all budgets is dotted along the coast. Watersports of all types are available, and trips can be arranged to the nearby secluded islands of Bidan, Telur and Song Song, which offer snorkelling, scuba diving and fishing.

BATIK

The Yahong Art Gallery on Batu Feringghi shows a collection of Batik paintings by members of the Teng Family (Chuah Thean Teng is considered to be the founder of the Malaysian tradition of batik painting). The gallery also has examples of fine art and crafts from Malaysia and China.

There are three batik factories in the area – Craft Batik is signposted from Teluk Bahang (but prices are high).

Penang at a Glance

BEST TIMES TO VISIT

Penang can be visited all year round. You might be interested to catch the Chinese Chingay festival in Mar or the Penang Regatta in Nov.

GETTING THERE

Penang is accessible by air, train and bus from the other cities. To get to the mainland at Butterworth, take the ferry. There is a toll if you are taking a car across the bridge.

GETTING AROUND

Taxis do not operate on meters, so agree your fare before boarding; trishaws charge a minimum rate per mile: agree on the price before boarding. The best way to get round the island is to hire a car.

WHERE TO STAY

Luxury
Bayview Beach Resort, Batu Feringghi, tel (04) 81112123, fax (04) 812140.
Penang Mutiara Beach Resort, Teluk Bahang, Batu Feringghi, tel (04) 812828. At the quieter end of the beach; seafood restaurant, **The Catch**, serves excellent food with nightly cultural shows.
Rasa Sayang Resort, Batu Feringghi, tel (04) 811811, fax (04) 811984, and its sister hotel the **Golden Sands**, tel (04) 811911, both in the Shangri-la Group.
Shangri-la Hotel, Jalan Magazine, tel 622622 (next to Komtar).

Mid-range
Eastern and Oriental, 10 Lebuh Farquhar, tel (04) 635322.
Grand Continental Hotel, 68 Jl Brick Kiln, Georgetown, tel (04) 636688, fax (04) 630299.
Lone Pine Hotel, 97 Batu Feringghi, tel (04) 811511, fax (04) 811282. One of the oldest hotels on Batu Feringghi.
Budget
Eastern Hotel, 509 Lbh Chulia, Georgetown, tel (04) 614597.
Hotel Fortuna, 406 Jl Penang, Georgetown, tel (04) 228 9282, fax (04) 371689.
Hotel Hong Ping, 273-B Lbh Chulia, Georgetown, tel (04) 625243.
Motel Sri Pantai, 516G Jl Hashim, Tanjung Bungah, tel (04) 890 9272.
White House Hotel, 72 Jl Penang, Georgetown, tel (04) 632385.

WHERE TO EAT

Most major hotels have excellent food outlets. The hawkers' food centre on Gurney Drive offers a wide variety of local food.
Dawood Restaurant, 63 Lbh Queen, Georgetown, tel (04) 611633: Indian Muslim, famous for its curries
Golden Gate Steamboat, Jl Cantonment, Georgetown, (04) 367509.
New Seaview Seafood Village, 551 Tanjung Bungah, tel (04) 806229.
Nonya Corner, 15 Jl Pahang, Georgetown, tel (04) 228 1412.
Tandoori House, 34 Lorong Hutton, Georgetown, tel (04) 619105: Moghul cuisine.
Tzechu-Lin Vegetarian Food Centre, 229C Jl Burmah, Georgetown, tel (04) 373357.

TOURS AND EXCURSIONS

City tours around Georgetown, round-island tour to see rural Penang and boat trips to nearby Pulau Bayar and Song Song. **Tourist Information Centre**, 3rd floor KOMTAR, Jl Penang, tel (04) 614461.

USEFUL CONTACTS

Malaysia Tourism Promotion Board (Northern Region), 10 Jl Tun Syed Sheh Barakbah, tel (04) 620066.
Penang Development Corporation, 1 Persiaran Mahsuri, Bandar Bayan Baru, 11909 Bayan Lepas, tel (04) 832111/832911, fax (04) 832405.

PENANG	J	F	M	A	M	J	J	A	S	O	N	D
AVERAGE TEMP. °F	80	80	82	82	82	80	80	80	80	78	80	80
AVERAGE TEMP. °C	27	27	28	28	28	27	27	27	27	26	27	27
Hours of Sun Daily	8	8	8	7	7	7	7	6	5	6	6	7
RAINFALL in	3	3	6	9	9	7	8	9	14	15	9	4
RAINFALL mm	69	72	146	221	230	178	192	242	356	383	232	114
Days of Rainfall	5	6	9	14	14	11	12	14	18	19	15	9

6
The East Coast

Blessed with miles of golden sand from Kelantan through Terengganu and Pahang down to parts of Johor, the East Coast offers the best beaches in Malaysia. Being fairly undeveloped compared with the West Coast, it has managed to retain its charm and unique Malay characteristics, with its coconut plantations and quaint villages on stilts. The unhurried pace of life on the East Coast makes it an ideal place for a relaxing holiday with just sun, sea and sand and the occasional cultural break in between the applications of suntan lotion.

KELANTAN

The northernmost of the East Coast states, Kelantan, whose name means 'Land of Lightning' shares a border with Thailand. In the early 1900s Kelantan was recognized as a tributary state of Thailand but in 1909 it was handed to the British. The state became part of the Federation of Malaya in 1948. During World War II **Kota Bharu**, the capital, witnessed the first landing of Japanese troops in the Peninsula in 1941.

Kota Bharu **

In Kelantan's capital, modern buildings sprout amongst landmarks of past eras and colourful trishaws still jostle with the traffic. For an insight into the strong traditions and culture of the Kelantanese, take a stroll through the 'Cultural Zone' along **Jalan Sultan** and **Jalan Hilir Kota** and the bustling **New Central Market**. Other attractions reflect the culture and religious nature of this state.

CLIMATE

The East Coast is subject to the monsoon season. The wet season is Nov–Mar when the northeast monsoon brings high wind and rain. The best time to visit the East Coast is mid-Mar–Oct when you can be assured of blue skies and calm seas.

Opposite: *Sunset over the South China Sea, off the Peninsula's peaceful East Coast.*

A banana seller in Kota Bharu's vibrant Central Market. Over 40 varieties of bananas are grown in Malaysia, from deliciously sweet pisang mas *or golden bananas to giant* pisang tanduk, *only edible when cooked.*

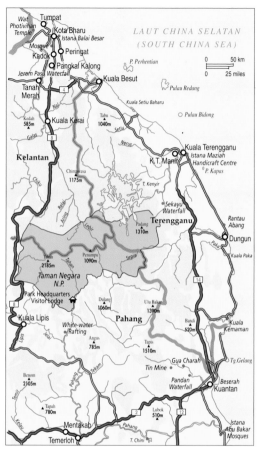

Malay Cultural Traditions

Kelantan is steeped in tradition and is the centre for Malay culture. At the **Gelanggang Seni**, the Kelantan Culture Centre in Jalan Mahmud, visitors can watch highly skilled **top spinners** hurling *gasing* (tops), the size of a dinner plate and weighing up to 5.5kg (12 lb), into a spin which may last as long as two hours! **Kite-flying** is another national pastime which dates back to the 1500s during the early days of the Melaka Sultanate. The *wau*, or kites, come in all shapes and colours and are made from bamboo and paper. The most popular shape is the *wau bulan* or 'moon kite', whose tailpiece resembles the crescent moon. A typical *wau bulan* measures up to 3.5m (11ft) from head to tail and is capable of soaring to great heights. Malaysia Airlines adopted it as their logo, as it symbolizes stability and controlled flight.

Drummers at Kelantan's annual drum festival playing rebana, *giant drums made from hollowed logs. Kampung teams of up to 12 men compete in tests of tone and rhythm.*

Theatre art plays an important part in Kelantanese culture. The most popular is *wayang kulit*, the shadow-puppet play, in which puppets made from buffalo hide mounted on bamboo sticks are cleverly manoeuvred behind a screen of white cloth with an oil lamp providing the light. Backed by a traditional orchestra, the *tok dalang* or puppeteer skilfully narrates the story, usually from the Hindu epics, and invariably the play ends with the triumph of good over evil.

Silvercraft is a thriving cottage industry in Kelantan. Silver fruit bowls, tea sets, ash trays, spoons, brooches and other jewellery are popular buys here in addition to **batik** in silk, cotton or rayon. This area is also famous for its *kain songket*, in which threads of gold and silver are woven into silk cloth used for weddings and other ceremonial occasions. This is a legacy handed down from the ancient court of Kelantan where silk from China and gold and silver thread from India were formerly woven exclusively for royalty. You can visit a *songket* workshop at Kampung Penambang near Kota Bharu.

The **New Central Market** in Kota Bharu exudes the real atmosphere of Malay life. The market-place is a hive of activity and colour as the traders, mostly women, sit in groups behind their displays of vegetables, fruits, cakes and coconuts, haggling and gossiping loudly while chewing at betel leaves.

> **THE EAST COAST: MUSLIM STRONGHOLD**
>
> It is important to note that the East Coast States of Malaysia are more conservative than the other parts of the country, as are the Islamic state governments. Kelantan, in particular, is the strictest of them all. Visitors should be sensitive to local tenets of modesty and public behaviour. Women should not be scantily clad, even on the beach, and topless sunbathing is strictly forbidden. The public display of intimacy between a man and a woman is frowned upon. Kelantan is also the only state which forbids the sale of alcohol in public places and in state-owned hotels.

Although the population of Kelantan is predominantly Malay, the Buddhist influence of Thailand extends over the border, especially in the northern district of Tumpat. Here in Kampung Jambu is the Buddhist temple of **Wat Phothivihan**, which was completed in 1980 and accommodates a reclining Buddha 40m (130ft) long: the largest in Southeast Asia.

Kelantan's Beaches **

Kelantan's sandy coast includes a beach whose original, rather suggestive, name of **Pantai Cinta Berahi** (the 'Beach of Passionate Love') has now officially been changed to **Pantai Cahaya Bulan** ('Moonlight Beach'). It is crowded at weekends and holidays. Further down the coast is **Pantai Dasar Sabak** where you can watch fishermen coming ashore in their ornately painted boats. At **Dalam Rhu** about 6km (3.5 miles) from Kota Bharu is the 'Beach of Whispering Breeze', ideal for snorkelling, scuba diving and fishing.

TERENGGANU

There is a story that Terengganu derived its name from an early traveller who saw a light on the distant shore and called out *'Terang'* (which means 'light'), to which his companion replied *'Anu?'* (meaning 'where'). This stretch of golden coast which stretches all the way to Pahang is synonymous with unspoilt beaches, clear blue skies and warm emerald seas rich with marine life, particularly around the numerous small islands off the coast. From **Kuala Besut** in the northern part of the state to **Kemaman** in the south, the coast is dotted with typical Malay villages surrounded by swaying coconut trees and goats, cows and chickens roaming freely.

Soft white sand lapped by clear blue sea characterizes the beautiful beaches around the islands off the coast of Terengganu, which also have some of the best dive sites in Malaysia. This beach is on Pulau Redang.

Kuala Terengganu *

The state capital of Terengganu is a former fishing village, and the centre of activity is still the busy waterfront. The market sells an abundance of seafood in the early morning. The **Genlanggang Seni** (cultural centre) is housed in one of the town's traditional carved Malay houses; it stages performances of traditional dance and games. Trishaws are still a popular mode of transport.

The Coastal Resorts ***

Although there are numerous modest beach resorts, there are only three international standard resorts in this area. The **Primula Beach Resort** in Kuala Terengganu has a lovely garden, swimming pool and beach, but its atmosphere is less relaxing and the beach is not so good or clean as those outside the town. Just north of Kuala Terengganu is the brand new **Sutra Beach Resort** at Kampung Rhu Tapai near the village of Merang (not to be confused with **Marang**, a picturesque fishing village further south). The tranquil 121-chalet resort is built on a secluded beach, within easy reach of some of the finest diving sites on the East Coast at **Pulau Redang**, **Pulau Bidong** and **Pulau Perhentian**. This resort offers coaching in scuba diving and is planning to develop some chalet accommodation on Pulau Redang.

Near the town of Dungun is the delightful resort of **Tanjung Jara**, like an old Malay palace set in large, beautifully landscaped gardens with a swimming pool by a small stream where giant monitor lizards saunter freely. The garden sweeps onto one of the best beaches on the East Coast. A few minutes' drive away is **Rantau Abang** where between May and September you may be treated to a sight of giant leatherback turtles coming ashore to lay their eggs. This beach is one of only six in the world visited by these rare and gentle giants. There is a Turtle Information Centre here, tel (09) 844169.

About 6km (4 miles) and 30 minutes by regular boat service from the fishing village of Marang is **Pulau Kapas**, renowned for its clear water and marine life. **Pulau Tenggol**, 17km (11 miles) off the village of Kuala

LEATHERBACK TURTLES

The leatherback turtle (*Dermochelys coriacea*) is the largest marine turtle, and one of the largest reptiles, in the world. They can grow up to 3m (10ft) in length and are said to live for hundreds of years. The females who lay their eggs on Rantau Abang beach will return to the same stretch of beach year after year, spending the rest of their time far out in the Pacific Ocean. They arrive on shore between May and September (mostly in June and July), sometimes making several visits during this time, each laying up to 150 eggs in a pit laboriously scooped in the sand.

A very small percentage of the eggs end up as mature turtles: they are in danger from predators on land, and many small turtles are caught by gulls or fish once they reach the sea. Egg collection by humans over many years has seriously depleted their numbers, as has marine pollution and fishing with large drift nets in which they become entangled.

The day's catch is set neatly out to dry in the sun at Beserah.

Dungun, is cloaked in luxuriant forest rich in wildlife, particularly reptiles. Tours to the island can be booked through Tanjung Jara Beach Resort or you can arrange with the local fishermen to ferry you there for a small fee.

Exploring inland

For those seeking adventure, the **Sekayu Recreational Park**, 56km (35 miles) from Kuala Terengganu is the ideal place. The park is set in primeval forest with cascading waterfalls and natural pools ideal for swimming. There are chalets, picnic areas and changing rooms for day trippers. **Kenyir Lake**, 55km (34 miles) from Kuala Terengganu, offers a peaceful sanctuary for picnics and nature walks. The lake, formed by the Kenyir Dam, is a haven for fishing enthusiasts. Boats can be hired from local fishermen.

PAHANG

Pahang is the largest state in Peninsular Malaysia and bears all the hallmarks of a great holiday destination. It almost monopolizes the major places of interest in the Peninsula – superb **beaches**, **Taman Negara**, **Pulau Tioman** and the three top hill resorts (for details of the latter, see Chapter 3). **Kuantan**, the state capital, is a nondescript town but an ideal launch-pad from which to explore the state.

Seaside Villages ★★★

Only 5km (3 miles) from Kuantan is **Teluk Chempedak**, a popular beach with plenty of accommodation and restaurants, and craft shops specializing in batik. A short trek through the **Teluk Chempedak Forest Reserve** will lead you to the secluded **Teluk Pelindung**. Nearby is the picturesque little fishing village of **Beserah**. Here you will be able to see water buffaloes transporting fish from the sea to the ramshackle factory on the beach which produces the *ikan bilis* (anchovies) for which this area is famous. North of Beserah is **Kampung Balok** which is the ideal spot for windsurfing. The **Coral Beach Resort** dominates this stretch of the beach but there are a number of smaller resorts around the area. Further up the coast is **Kampung Cherating**, 47km (29 miles) from Kuantan, which is normally associated with Club Méditerranée, although this resort occupies only a fraction of the vast expanse of beach. About 1.5km (1 mile) from Cherating is **Chendor Beach** where green turtles come ashore to lay eggs.

Gua Charah ★

Venturing inland about 25km (16 miles) northwest from Kuantan at **Panching**, Gua

GUNUNG TAHAN

At 2187m (7175ft), Gunung Tahan is the highest mountain in the Peninsula. The trek from Park Headquarters to the summit takes five days, plus four for the return journey; you must be accompanied by a guide.

Charah is a series of limestone caves which are revered as a Buddhist sanctuary. In one of the caves, a 9m (30ft) long reclining Buddha has been carved out of the solid rock. There are monks in residence in the temple. Visitors may explore deep into the gorges. The nearby **Sungai Pandan Waterfalls** cascade into a big pool which is perfect for a dip after a long trek.

Tasek Chini *

Travel south to **Kampung Belimbing**, about 100km (63 miles) from Kuantan, to take a boat through a series of 12 picturesque lakes carpeted with lotus blossoms from June to September. This is the legendary Tasek Chini. It is said that an ancient Khmer walled city once existed here. The Jakuns, one of the Orang Asli tribes who live by the lake, believe that a giant monster, the Naga, still guards its depths. Tasek Chini has a number of wooden chalets and campsites to cater for overnight visitors.

Taman Negara ***

For the ultimate experience of the oldest rainforest in the world, undisturbed for about 130 million years, hike up to the largest national park in West Malaysia. Taman Negara covers an area of 4343km² (1700 sq miles). This park was designated in 1938 for the purpose of propagation, protection and preservation of the indigenous flora and fauna. To appreciate it fully, a stay of two to four

Left: *A view across the canopy of the undisturbed forest of Taman Negara shows how the whole of Malaysia's interior once appeared.*
Below: *Lotus flowers cover the water of Tasek Chini from June to September.*

Above: *A secluded beach on Pulau Tioman, one of the most beautiful tropical islands in the world.*
Opposite: *The Abu Bakar Mosque, facing the Straits of Johor.*

days is recommended. For the botanist, there is an extensive range of vegetation from the lowland dipterocarp forests and swamp forests to the oaks and dwarf upper montane flora near the summit region of **Gunung Tahan**. The wildlife enthusiast will find an abundance of fauna. There are six wildlife hides in the park, all built overlooking salt-licks and grassy clearings. Due to the density of the vegetation, however, sightings of the animals can be difficult. From hides deep in the interior, large animals like the *seladang* (wild ox), sambar and barking deer, wild pigs and tapirs can be seen. Elephants, leopards, tigers, sun bears and Sumatran rhinoceros are present but are rarely seen by visitors. Over 250 species of birds have been recorded here. The park also maps out jungle treks of various durations from one to nine days: you must be accompanied by guides on long treks.

Pulau Tioman ★★★

The island of Tioman lies off the southern coast of Pahang. What it lacks in size, measuring only 39km (25 miles) long and 19km (12 miles) at its widest, it makes up in beauty. It is surrounded by sparkling blue waters teeming with marine life and beaches of fine golden sand. It gained international fame when it was chosen as the location for the film *South Pacific* in the 1950s. This is one of the most popular islands off the East Coast for scuba diving and snorkelling. The shallow waters at **Salang Beach** and around the nearby islands of **Tulai** and **Renggis** offer the best diving spots. Tioman's interior is equally spectacular, with lofty mountains, lush tropical forests and quaint villages. Tourists easily outnumber the local inhabitants at the height of the season. There are jungle treks traversing the island from **Juara** to **Tekek**, and for those reluctant to walk, sea buses will transport you round the island. Check the timetable at the bars in the main resorts.

SINGAPORE

The little diamond-shaped island of Singapore occupies a strategic position at the southern tip of the Malay Pensinula, on the shortest marine route between the Indian Ocean and the South China Sea. Its future was assured in 1819, when it was chosen by Thomas Stamford Raffles as the site for a trading post for the British East India Company. At that time its population numbered about 150 – five years later it had risen to over 10,000. The current population is some 2.7 million, three-quarters of whom are Chinese. Raffles' trading post is now one of the richest countries in Asia.

JOHOR

When the Portuguese invaded the Melaka sultanate in 1511, the sultan and his court fled to Johor and set up a new kingdom. **Johor Bahru**, the present capital, is a modern city and the gateway to Malaysia from the south. Accessed by the 1km (half mile) causeway over the **Johor Straits**, the people of Singapore virtually use Johor Bahru (it is known locally as 'JB') as an extension of the island for shopping and eating out, especially in the seafood restaurants. Hence weekend traffic on the causeway is very congested. Places of interest in the city include the **Istana Besar** (Grand Palace) and the **Royal Abu Bakar Museum** along Jalan Tun Dr Ismail. Built in 1866 by Sultan Abu Bakar, it is the oldest building in the city and today is a museum exhibiting his possessions. The beautifully landscaped gardens of the Grand Palace spread over 54ha (133 acres) of land. The present sultan's residence is the **Istana Bukit Serene**, with a spectacular 32m (100ft) tower. Its superb grounds feature the sultan's orchid gardens and collection of vintage cars. The garden is open to the public. Not far from the Grand Palace is the imposing **Sultan Abu Bakar Mosque**.

Most of Johor is devoted to pineapple and palm oil plantations, rubber estates and industry. **Mersing** on the east coast is a bustling fishing town and is the setting-off point for Pulau Tioman and Johor's **Marine Park**, a cluster of seven islands surrounded by clear blue seas, fine white sandy beaches and rich marine life. Most of the islands offer very basic accommodation in wooden chalets. **Kukup**, a village on the tip of the southwest coast, is worth a visit for its seafood restaurants built into the sea on stilts. The prawns and chilli crab dishes here are famous and it is a popular stop for tourists on package tours from Singapore (it gets very crowded at weekends).

SULTAN ABU BAKAR

Regarded as the father of modern Johor, Abu Bakar pronounced himself raja in 1868. A polo-playing anglophile, he had received an English education in Singapore, and made several trips to the British court, befriending Queen Victoria, who recognized him as sultan of Johor in 1885. He developed the state's economy and drew up its written constitution, carefully remaining independent of British rule. Johor was the last state to join the Malay Federation in 1914.

East Coast at a Glance

BEST TIMES TO VISIT

Dry season from Apr–Oct. From Nov–Mar the East Coast is subject to heavy rains of northeast monsoon: **Taman Negara** is closed from 15 Nov to 14 Jan.

GETTING THERE

Daily flights on Malaysia Airlines to **Kota Bharu** and **Kuala Terengganu** from KL, Penang and Johor. Access by sea to **Pulau Tioman** is from Mersing in Johor. Daily flights from KL by Pelangi Air. **Kuantan** is easily accessible, with daily flights and air-conditioned express bus services from KL.
Johor Bharu is well served by air, road and rail from KL, Singapore and Penang. Journey to **Taman Negara** starts at Jerantut (4hr drive from KL) to Kuala Tembeling with a 59km (37 miles) boat journey up the Tembeling River to Park Headquarters at Kuala Tahan.

GETTING AROUND

Taxis and local buses operate in and between the East Coast states. Cars can be hired in **Kota Bharu**, **Terengganu** and **Kuantan**. Kampungs and beaches on **Pulau Tioman** are reached by boat or by forest trail.

WHERE TO STAY

Kelantan
Luxury
Hotel Perdana, Jl Mahmud, P O Box 222, Kota Bharu, tel (09) 748 5000, fax (09) 744 7621.
Perdana Beach Resort, Pa'amat, Pantai Cahaya Bulan, P O Box 121, Jl Kuala, Kota Bharu, tel (09) 733000, fax (09) 739980.
Mid-range
Juita Inn, 60-64 Jl Pintu Pong, Kota Bharu, tel (09) 744 6888, fax (09) 744 5777.
Kencana Inn, Lot 177-181, Jl Padang Garong, Kota Bharu, tel (09) 744 7944, fax (09) 744 0181.
Budget
Hotel Aman, 236 C-D Jl Tengku Besar, Kota Bharu, tel (09) 744 3049.
Windmill Guesthouse, Jl Pengkalan Chepa, Kota Bharu, tel (09) 773113.

Terengganu
Luxury
Primula Beach Resort, Jl Persinggahan, P O Box 43, Kuala Terengganu, tel (09) 622100, fax (09) 633360.
Sutra Beach Resort, Kampung Rhu Tapai, Merang, 22100 Setiu Terengganu, tel (09) 669 6200, fax (09) 669 6410.
Tanjung Jara Beach Hotel, 8th Mile Off Dungun, Dungun, tel (09) 841801, fax (09) 842653.
Mid-range
Qurata Riverside Resort, Lot 175K Kuala Ibai, Kuala Terengganu, tel (09) 675590, fax (09) 675511.
Rantau Abang Visitor Centre (for turtle watch), 13th Mile Off Dungun, Dungun, tel (09) 841533.
River Garden Hotel, K-114 Jl Sulaiman, Kemaman, tel (09) 596322, fax (09) 596323.
Budget
City Hotel, 97-99 Jl Banggol, Kuala Terengganu, tel (09) 621481.
Hotel Marina Kemaman, K 307 & 308 Jl Che Teng, Kemaman, tel (09) 591241.
Penarik Inn, Lot 31, Kampung Penarik Baru, Wakil Pos, Penarik, 22121 Permaisuri, Setiu. 'Home-stay' in A-frame huts, simple fishermen's huts or family size tents. Meals served under thatched canopy on beach. No telephone. Write to Mr Baharuddin at above address.
Pulau Kapas Garden Resort, Pulau Kapas, Marang, tel/fax (09) 635533.
Hotel Sura, 263 E & F Jl Bahru, Dungun, tel (09) 841716.

Pahang
Luxury
Hyatt Kuantan, Teluk Chempedak, Kuantan, tel (09) 513 1234, fax (09) 513 7577.
Impiana Resort Cherating, Kilometer 31, Jl Kuantan-Kemaman, Kuantan, tel (09) 439000, fax (09) 439090.
Merlin Inn Resort Kuantan, Peti Surat 46, Teluk Chempedak, Kuantan, tel (09) 514 1388, fax (09) 513 3001.
Mid-range
Hotel Pacific, 60-62 Jl Bukit Ubi, Kuantan. tel (09) 514 1890, fax (09) 514 1979.
Hotel Samura Riverview, Jl

East Coast at a Glance

Besar, Kuantan, tel (09) 555333, fax (09) 500618.
Tanjung Gelang Motel, 15km Balok Beach, Kuantan, tel (09) 587254.
Le Village Beach Resort, Lot 1260 Sungai Karang, Beserah, Kuantan, tel (09) 587900, fax (09) 587899.
Budget
Hotel Beserah, 2 Jl Beserah, Kuantan, tel (09 526144.
Moonlight Hotel, 50-52 Jl Teluk Sisek, Kuantan, tel (09) 524277.
Hotel New Wing Yuen, 63-65 Jl Bukit Ubi, Kuantan, tel (09) 513 1548.
There are numerous simple chalets and 'home-stays' with village families.

Pulau Tioman
Luxury
Berjaya Tioman Beach Resort, Lalang; sales office: PO Box 4, Mersing, Johor, tel (09) 445445, fax (09) 445718.
Mid-range – Budget
ABC Beach, Kg Genting, tel (011) 349868.
Mastura Chalets, Kg Tekek, tel (011) 714454.
Nazri's Place, Kg Air Batang, tel (011) 349534.
Salang Indah, Kg Salang, tel (011) 730230.
Samudra Swiss Cottage, Kg Tekek, tel (07) 248728.
Tioman Paya Resort, Kg Paya; reservations (Mersing): tel (07) 792602/792169, fax (07) 792603.

WHERE TO EAT

Kelantan

Choo Choon Huay Restaurant, 149 Jl Post Office Lama, Kota Bharu, tel (09) 781720.
Malaysia Restoran, 398F Jl Sultan Zainab, Kota Bharu, tel (09) 783398.
Satay Indera Restoran, Jl Perkeliling, Kota Bharu, tel (09) 748498.
Sun Too Restaurant & Snack, 782-AB Jl Temonggong, Kota Bharu, tel (09) 782252.

Terengganu
Restoran Awana Sea Food, Jl Kelab Kerajaan, Kuala Terengganu, tel (09) 633309.
Delima Restaurant, 83 Jl Paya Bunga, Kuala Terengganu, tel (09) 292162.
Good Luck Restoran, 11K Jl Kota Lama, Kuala Terengganu, tel (09) 627573.

Pahang
Bunga Raya Restoran, A1124 Jl Telok Sisek, Kuantan, tel (09) 523770.
Golden Sea Food Restaurant, B-2616 Jl Beserah, Kuantan, tel (09) 522148.
Meena Curry House, C714G Jl Dato Lim Hoe Teck, Kuantan, tel (09) 504824.

TOURS AND EXCURSIONS

Kelantan and Terengganu: Trips to Pulau Perhentian, Redang, Bidong and Kapas for snorkelling and scuba diving. Tours to Kain Songket factory and beach resorts.
Taman Negara: All bookings must be made in advance at the Taman Negara KL office, tel (03) 2610393, fax (03) 2610615, or Kuala Tahan office, tel (09) 263500, fax (09) 261500.

USEFUL CONTACTS

Malaysia Tourism Promotion Board (East Coast Region), 2243 Ground Floor, Wisma MCIS, Kuala Terengganu, tel (09) 621893, fax (09) 621791.
Kelantan Tourist Information Centre, Jl Ibrahim, Kota Bharu, tel (09) 783543.
Culture, Art & Tourism Division of Terengganu, 9th Floor, Wisma Darul Iman, Kuala Terengganu, tel (09) 631957.
Pahang Industrial & Tourism Division, 14th Floor, Kompleks Teruntum, Jl Mahkota, Kuantan, tel (09) 522346.
The Tourist Centre, Mersing, Johor, tel (09) 791204.

KUANTAN	J	F	M	A	M	J	J	A	S	O	N	D
AVERAGE TEMP. °F	77	77	78	80	80	80	78	78	78	78	77	77
AVERAGE TEMP. °C	25	25	26	27	27	27	26	26	26	26	25	25
Hours of Sun Daily	5	6	7	7	7	6	7	6	6	5	4	4
RAINFALL in	12	6	7	6	8	6	7	7	9	10	14	22
RAINFALL mm	296	142	178	164	203	160	172	174	233	272	344	564
Days of Rainfall	12	9	9	11	12	9	11	11	14	16	19	18

7
Sarawak

Known as 'The Land of the Hornbills', Sarawak, the largest of the thirteen states of Malaysia, sprawls across the northwestern part of the island of **Borneo**. Whilst its sister states in West Malaysia are predominantly Malay, Sarawak is characterized by the distinctive ethnic culture of its indigenous tribes. It has the most diverse populace in the country with more than 25 ethnic communities, including migrant Indonesians and Indians. Its savage and colourful history might have come straight out of a romantic Victorian novel: a young swashbuckling Englishman setting sail to the wilds of Borneo, fighting pirates and fierce head-hunters, and eventually becoming the country's first **'White Rajah'**. Its wild terrain of rugged mountains and rainforest covering three-quarters of the land makes Sarawak one of the best places for adventure holidays. If you are looking for high-rise buildings, large shopping malls and all the trappings of modern resorts, then it is not recommended. Sarawak takes tourism at its own pace, with a heavy emphasis on its rich colourful tribal culture and to a lesser extent its colonial past.

Sarawak became a state in its own right when it was handed over as a fief by the sultan of Brunei to a young English trader, **James Brooke**, seeking adventure and fortune in the East. Quite by chance he arrived in Sarawak where he helped to quell a local rebellion and as a reward was officially installed as 'rajah' of Sarawak on 18 September 1842. He ruled Sarawak well, bringing law and order to the country by fighting piracy and

CLIMATE

The rainy season runs from the end of Oct–Mar, but towards the end of the dry season river levels may fall sufficiently to make them impassable by boat: the best time to visit is therefore Mar–Jun. As elsewhere in Malaysia, the temperature remains fairly constant, rarely dropping below 20°C (68°F) at night, and humidity is usually about 80%.

Opposite: *The rhinoceros hornbill, called* kenyalang *by the Iban, is the state bird of Sarawak. It is the largest of the hornbills of Borneo.*

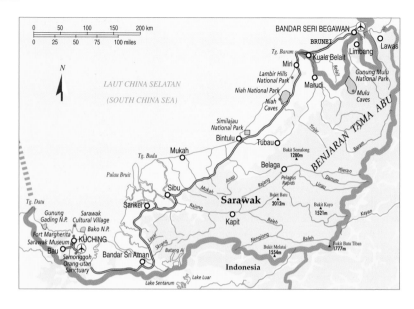

head-hunting. He died in 1868 and was succeeded by his nephew, Charles Brooke, who set up a formal government administration. While his uncle had had a difficult task fighting pirates and quelling tribal rebellion and Chinese uprisings, Charles concentrated on economic development of the country. Rajah Charles Brooke died in 1917 and his second son, Charles Vyner Brooke, became the third and last Rajah of Sarawak. In 1941, while Rajah Vyner Brooke was on holiday in Australia, the Japanese occupied Sarawak. Much of the economic infrastructure was disrupted and destroyed. For four years the country suffered extreme oppression and hardship and most of the European officers in Sarawak were rounded up and interned in prison camps. Many died during their ordeal. After the liberation in 1945, Rajah Brooke, realizing that he would not have the resources to restore the country, decided to relinquish his power and ceded Sarawak to Britain. On 1 July 1946, Sarawak became a British Crown Colony, until in 1963 it joined Malaysia.

KUCHING

The name of Sarawak's capital means 'cat' in Malay. Some sources claim that the town was named after the *mata kuching* (cats' eyes trees) which grow in abundance in the area. The city today is affectionately known as 'Cat City' and even has its own cat museum, located in the new city hall in Petra Jaya. Kuching is small enough for visitors to reach its main places of interest on foot.

Sarawak Museum ★★★

This world-famous museum is a good place to start your tour, as it has one of the finest ethnological collections in Southeast Asia, as well as examples of Bornean wildlife and colonial relics. The new wing at Dewan Abdul Razak concentrates on models of ethnic dwellings and crafts, and includes a replica of Niah Great Cave with its stone-age relics. The museum opens from 09:15 to 17:30 from Monday to Thursday and 09:15 to 18:00 on Saturday and Sunday. It is closed on Friday. Admission is free.

The Legacy of the White Rajahs ★★★

A short walk into town along Jalan Tun Haji Openg brings you to the city's historic centre. But for the tropical heat and the people, you could easily be fooled into thinking you were in a British city. The indelible legacy of the Brooke period is evident in the imposing **General Post Office** built in Renaissance style in 1931. The Brooke emblem of a badger with the inscription *Dum spiro, spero* ('While I live, I hope') is displayed on the pediment. Directly opposite the post office is the **Pavilion**, which has been described as looking like a cake with white icing. It was originally the General Hospital. The **Round**

THE PEOPLE OF SARAWAK

Sarawak's population of 1.7 million living in an area of 124,967 km² (48,815 sq miles) makes it a very sparsely inhabited state, with most settlements concentrating in the coastal region and along the banks of the numerous rivers which criss-cross the country. The Iban form the largest group, followed by the Chinese and Malays. Other indigenous groups include the Kayan and Kenyah tribes who inhabit the banks of the upper Baram and Rajang Rivers; the Kelabit, hill-rice growers from the highlands around Bareo; the Bidayuh, in the area around Kuching; the Melanau, the original coastal people of Sarawak; and the nomadic Penan. Head-hunting is now confined to the recruitment agencies of the corporate world of big Malaysian companies.

Sunset over the Sarawak River at Kuching.

BURIED ALIVE

In front of the new Sarawak Museum stands a double-pole wooden structure with a coffin-like top, intricately carved with designs of fearsome faces and stylized animals. This is the burial pole, called the *klirieng*, of a chief of the Kajang, an Orang Ulu tribe. The old burial custom involved placing the bones of the deceased in a jar on top of the structure. Before the *klirieng* was erected, a slave would be thrown into the pit as a sacrifice or tied to the burial pole and left to die. The belief was that the slave would accompany his master to serve him in the next world. This ritual was restricted to the aristocrats of the Orang Ulu and Melanau tribes.

Tower, next to the Pavilion, was built in 1886 as a dispensary. Its twin round towers command an unimpeded view of the main avenues leading to the town centre, and it is thought that the Rajah might have intended to use it as a watch tower in an emergency. Across a courtyard is the **Court House**, erected in 1874. The building is raised slightly above ground, possibly to avoid floodwater from the river. At the front of the Court House is a clocktower with a balcony from which the Rajahs used to address their subjects. In front of the building is the Charles Brooke memorial obelisk which was completed in 1924.

Across the road on the river-bank is the **Square Tower**, built in 1879 in late Renaissance style. During the days of the Rajahs it was used, in an unlikely combination of functions, as a fortress and occasionally as a ballroom. One of the most magnificent buildings of the Brooke era is the **Astana** (Palace), now the home of the Governor of Sarawak. Built in 1870 by Rajah Charles Brooke for his bride, the Ranee Margaret, the palace stands on a rolling hill on the northern bank of the Sarawak River, facing the Main Bazaar. It is not open to the public but you may visit the beautiful grounds. There is a regular sampan service ferrying passengers across the river. The castellated **Fort Margherita** is near the Astana. Named after, and designed by, Ranee Margaret, it was built in 1879 and commands a strategic position on a hill overlooking the river. It is now a police museum, housing a display of firearms confiscated from gangsters and guerrillas, execution methods of the Brooke era and even a cluster of skulls from the head-hunting days of the Iban.

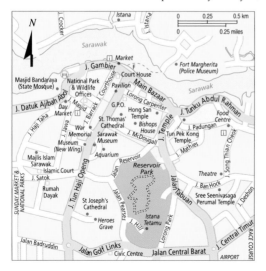

Main Bazaar ★★

Along the river front are some of the oldest Chinese shophouses in the country, which make for a fascinating stroll along the 'five-foot way'. The Sarawak Tourist Association is situated along here. Further down the road at **Jalan Gambier** are some dilapidated shophouses owned by Indian traders, selling mainly spices. Between them is a very narrow alleyway leading to one of the oldest mosques in the country. It was built by Indian Muslims in the mid-19th century. Indian textile shops on this lane sell silk and other fine fabrics. The lane will lead you to Jalan India, which has recently been closed to traffic. It is a delightful place to shop for fabrics and haggling is expected. A walk to the end of Jalan India will lead you to the open air market by the bus terminal and taxi stand. It is the oldest eating place in the city and houses several food stalls. Opposite the Main Bazaar is the brand new Waterfront esplanade. The once dilapidated river-bank has now been transformed into a beautiful promenade with musical fountains and gardens. There are food stalls, restaurants and an amphitheatre. It is a pleasant way to spend an evening watching the local colour.

Perched on the bank of the Sarawak River near the open air market on Jalan Mesjid is the splendid State Mosque built in 1968 on the site of an old wooden mosque. In front is the old Muslim cemetery. At the far end of the Main Bazaar is the Chinese community's principal place of worship, the Tua Pek Kong Temple. Built in 1876 on a hill facing the river, it is a gaudy structure of bright red walls with a very ornate blue roof festooned with mythological figures. This temple is famous for the Wang Kang celebration in commemoration of the dead.

The district of Kuching on the northern bank of the Sarawak River mainly consists of Malay kampungs. Prominent on its hilltop site is Fort Margherita, built in 1870 like an English castle, complete with battlements and a turret.

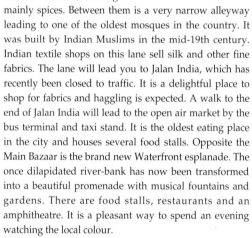

GUARDIAN OF KUCHING

Although there had been a fort on the site since 1841, an Iban raid on Kuching from the river in 1878 prompted its rebuilding with battlements and a watchtower. Fort Margherita never had to be used defensively, but a sentry was posted on the tower every night throughout the remaining years of the Brookes' rule. He had to shout 'All's well' on the hour all through the night, and his reassuring call could be heard by the rajah in the Astana.

Above: *The view from a beach on the Santubong peninsula north of Kuching, with another part of the coast of Sarawak in the distance.* **Opposite**: *The sandstone cliffs along the coast of Bako National Park have been carved into spectacular natural shapes.*

PUA KUMBU

Iban women are skilled weavers, and the highest test of this prized and ancient art is the pua kumbu, a ceremonial hanging. An ikat technique is employed – the warp threads are tie-dyed using colours extracted from forest plants – and the designs are passed down from one generation to the next. Many are stylized versions of birds, animals or plants. Some motifs represent mythical subjects and have a spiritual significance.

EXCURSIONS FROM KUCHING

There are two beach resorts about 45 minutes' drive from Kuching city centre, **Damai Beach Resort** and **Santubong Resort**. The four-star international standard Damai Beach Resort has its own private beach. Guests from the Holiday Inn Kuching can make use of the facilities at Damai Beach but a prior arrangement must be made with the hotel. The more modest Santubong Resort is a new establishment more geared to the local market. There is an 18-hole golf course adjacent to the hotel. For those who want a more rustic holiday, Camp Permai is the place. A few minutes' walk from Damai Beach, the main feature here is outward bound activity with jungle trekking, rock climbing, mountain climbing, overland expeditions, night hikes, zip towering and watersports.

Mini Sarawak ★★★

One tourist attraction not to be missed, adjacent to Damai Beach Resort, is the Sarawak Cultural Village. Built on a site of 7ha (17 acres), it contains seven representative ethnic houses: longhouses of the Bidayuh, Iban and Orang Ulu, a Penan Hut, a beautiful traditional wooden Melanau house (now the only such building in Sarawak), a Malay house and a Chinese farmhouse. Each group is represented by craftspeople demonstrating their various traditional skills. The village has a restaurant, souvenir shops and a theatre with a daily multicultural show at 14:00 featuring all the ethnic dances from the state accompanied by traditional instruments. The Cultural Village opens at 09:00 daily and closes at 17:30. It is highly recommended if you do not have the time to travel throughout Sarawak to see the 'real thing'.

Bako National Park ★★★

Situated 37km (23 miles) from Kuching is the first national park in Sarawak. Its coastline is dotted with beautiful sandy coves and strange rock formations with spectacular colours like pieces of abstract art. It has a very diverse vegetation and several jungle trails are carefully mapped out for visitors. You may encounter wildlife at close range, especially proboscis monkeys, bearded pigs, giant monitor lizards and macaques, who often steal belongings and food if left unattended on the beach. Beware! Bako has simply furnished bungalows and chalets for rent for overnight stays, and there is a small canteen selling groceries and Malaysian food. A permit to visit the park can be obtained from the Sarawak National Park booking office at the Sarawak Tourist Information Centre in Main Bazaar, or at the Bako boat terminal.

Longhouse Safari ***

A visit to a longhouse is best organized through local tour operators who will arrange transport, a guide and board and lodging in the longhouse. Travelling independently can be expensive as you have to charter your own boat. There are a few longhouses which welcome visitors in the Skrang River, Lemanak and Ulu Ai areas, all about six to eight hours' journey by car and boat from Kuching. Most tour operators offer resthouses, with basic facilities, near the longhouse.

It is important to remember that, when visiting a longhouse, you are a guest and you should respect the customs of the tribal people. Always remove your shoes when entering a longhouse and never refuse the tradi-

LONGHOUSES OF SARAWAK

The longhouse is the traditional dwelling of the Iban, Bidayuh and Orang Ulu. It is the oldest form of architecture in the country. The longhouse is built in a linear fashion under one roof and has a common hallway and verandah, but separate apartments for each of up to 80 families. There is usually one main exit and fearsome faces or motifs such as stylized dogs (as in the case of the Kayan and Kenyah longhouse) are carved on the door to frighten evil spirits away. The building of a longhouse involves a strict ritual of sacrifices of food to the earth spirits. The site chosen is usually by a river for water supply, fishing and transport and on high ground for defence purposes. Each longhouse is ruled by a chieftain (*tuai rumah*) who presides over social and judicial matters. Old war trophies of human skulls, reminders of the savage days of headhunting, hang in clusters over the rafters in the gallery in order to ward off evil spirits.

An Iban warrior, in feathered head-dress and silver jewellery, performing a traditional dance at a cultural performance in Kuching.

tonal drink of *tuak* (rice wine) when it is offered, even if you do not drink: just a token sip will suffice. Here you will be able to mingle with retired head-hunters – indicated by the tattoos on their knuckles and their throats, the ensigns of warriors. Some longhouses put on a performance of traditional dancing at night and it will please your hosts if you participate in the dancing and merry-making. It is customary to bring small gifts of sweets and biscuits for the children and cigarettes for the adults. Materials such as exercise books, pens and pencils, things that we take for granted in the modern world, are also greatly appreciated. If you are planning to visit a longhouse, be prepared to rough it, but the thrill of the adventure, the experience of being in a longhouse and the natural beauty of the scenery *en route* make it unforgettable.

Batang Ai ★★★

If you feel the real thing would be too much for you, you can go for a 'soft adventure' journey to **Batang Ai Longhouse Resort**, four hour's drive from Kuching followed by a 15-minute boat ride across a beautiful lake. It is fashioned after the traditional longhouse of the Iban, though each room is air-conditioned. Amenities include a bar, lounge and a restaurant featuring regular cultural performances. The lake can be used for fishing and canoeing. Day trips by boat to authentic longhouses can be arranged at the resort.

Semengoh Orang-utan Sanctuary ★★★

Nature lovers should not miss this reserve, 22km (14 miles) from Kuching on the road to Serian. A permit to visit must be obtained from the Sarawak Tourist Information Office in Main Bazaar or from the Forestry Department in Jalan Mosque. The sanctuary is a rehabilitation centre for orang-utans rescued from captivity or wounded by hunters. One such victim was 'Bullet', a 'twenty-something' male orang-utan who was the centre's star attraction until his death in April 1994. Rescued from the wild as an infant with a bullet in his head, he was found to have suffered brain damage and was

---

THE HORNBILL DANCE

This is the most famous of the dances performed in the longhouses of Sarawak. It probably originates with the Kayan and Kenyah people, who are accomplished musicians and dancers. The performers tie hornbill feathers to the ends of their fingers to accentuate the slow movements of the dance.

unable to cope in the wild. Other animals here include proboscis monkeys, gibbons, sun bears, hornbills and sea eagles. It is advisable to go during feeding times (08:30 to 09:00 and 14:30 to 15:00). Most of the orang-utans who return daily to feed are those newly released to the jungle who have not yet developed the habit of hunting for themselves, but some are just plain lazy scroungers!

An Iban longhouse built safely above flood level on the bank of the Rajang River. These days, corrugated iron is often used as roofing material in place of traditional palm thatch or ironwood shingles.

Sibu and the Rajang River *

The second largest town in Sarawak is a busy port at the mouth of the Rajang River, the longest river in Malaysia. This mighty river was once the scene of many a fierce battle among warring tribes. The Iban are mostly settled along the middle reaches of the river. In its upper stretches beyond Belaga, above the rapids, there are several longhouses belonging to Kayan, Kenyah and Kajang tribes, while the nomadic Penan still roam the forest deep in the interior.

NORTHERN SARAWAK

The gateway to northern Sarawak is the oil town of Miri. It is dominated by the Shell Petroleum company and a large number of the inhabitants are expatriates from the west. The town itself has not much to offer but the surroundings are outstanding.

SMALL BEGINNINGS

Miri's oil-boom began in 1910 when the country's first oil-well was drilled on Canada Hill, above the city, by Shell, then a small trading company exporting pepper and polished seashells and importing kerosene. The original well was finally shut down in 1972. The Miri field now produces 80 million barrels of oil a year.

NEEDLE-SHARP PEAKS

To the west of Gunung Mulu
rise the lesser peaks of
Gunung Api and Gunung
Benarat. Their lower slopes
are covered in dense forest.
Rising above the treetops on
Gunung Api are the spectacular limestone outcrops with
razor-sharp peaks known as
the Pinnacles. Excursions with
local guides can be arranged
to climb the Pinnacles (3
days/2 nights expedition with
a steep four-hour climb)
where on a clear day you will
be rewarded with a
panoramic view of the forest
stretching over to Brunei and
the South China Sea. The
rocks really are sharp and you
should take gloves and
strong boots to avoid cutting
yourself. Spenser St John,
who made the first attempt
to climb Gunung Mulu in
1856, described the Pinnacles
as 'the world's most night-
marish surface to travel over'.

Niah National Park **

The most famous attrac-
tion in the vicinity is this
3000ha (7500 acre)
National Park, about
130km (75 miles) south of
Miri. Here limestone for-
mations covering an area
of 11ha (27 acres) form the
Niah Great Cave where
world-renowned archaeo-
logical finds include a
37,000-year-old skull.
Nearby is **Kain Hitam** (the
Painted Cave). It was used
for prehistoric burials as is
evident from the remnants of boat-shaped coffins,
known as 'death ships', containing human remains,
watched over by paintings of little humanoid figures
drawn in red haematite on the walls. Today the caves are
home only to bats and edible-nest swiftlets. Intrepid collectors climb rickety bamboo scaffolding to gather the
nests. The caves are reached by a 45-minute trek on a
raised plankwalk meandering through the lowland forest which teems with birds and butterflies. A permit to
visit the Park must be obtained from the National Parks
and Wildlife Office in Wisma Pelita Tungku in Miri or
from the Sarawak Tourist Information Centre in
Kuching. Simple accommodation is available at the park
(must be pre-booked) and there is a resthouse at Batu
Niah, the nearest town to the caves.

Mulu National Park ***

This park is dominated by the sandstone mass of Gunung
Mulu which stands at 2376m (7794 ft) high, but the highlight of a journey to the park is the exploration of its awesome caves. Only four are open to the public. The **Deer
Cave** is reputed to be the largest cave passage in the
world. It is as high as it is wide, measuring 120m (393ft),
and is over 2km (1.25 miles) long. Millions of bats live in

the cave by day and they time-share it with the swiftlets who occupy it at night. It is an amazing spectacle to watch the interchange between the two species as the bats fly out of the cave like puffs of black smoke in a solid convoy while the swiftlets shriek impatiently to get in. To add to the chaos, bat hawks circle round the cave entrance to feast on the bats as they make their nightly exodus. This 'performance' happens every night at about 18:00.

Next to Deer Cave is **Lang's Cave**, the smallest of the four, but the most beautiful, with colourful stalactites, stalagmites and strange rock formations. The **Clearwater Cave** boasts the longest cave passage in Southeast Asia at 75km (47 miles) long, with an underground river and a maze of tunnels. A few hundred metres downriver is the **Cave of the Winds**, including a chamber of stalagmites resembling a throne and eerily human shapes, known as the King's Chamber. All four caves have steps, paths and plankwalks to allow visitors to explore in safety. For the more adventurous traveller, it is possible to explore deeper into the Clearwater Cave with a guide, but be prepared to wade chest-deep through under-

Opposite: *Inside the Great Cave at Niah where archaeological finds have shown that humans lived at least 37,000 years ago.*

Below: *The Deer Cave in Gunung Mulu National Park is the world's largest known cave passage.*

ground streams and crawl through small tunnels in pitch dark with only a torchlight or a miner's lamp to guide you. Not recommended for those who are not fit or who suffer from claustrophobia. The **Sarawak Chamber**, the largest known cave chamber in the world, which could easily accommodate forty 747 aircraft, is open only to experienced pot-holers on permitted expeditions. Trips to Mulu caves have to be accompanied by a park guide.

Sarawak at a Glance

The dry season is between Mar–Oct, though there is always the chance of occasional rain or thunderstorms. Gawai Dayak is celebrated on 1st June.

Kuching has several daily flights from Kuala Lumpur, Singapore and some direct flights from Hong Kong and Tokyo. It is also easily accessible worldwide via Kuala Lumpur or Singapore.

Buses and **taxis** operate within each town and in between the bigger towns. **River boats** are still a major means of transport in most rural areas. Travel to the **Bako** boat terminal by Petra Jaya bus or by taxi: from there take a boat to the park itself, or book the trip through local operators.
Express boat services
Concorde Pertama Union Express, 196 Jl Padungan, Kuching, tel (082) 414735 (Kuching-Sibu-Sarikei);
Hiap Tai Express, 50 Padungaan Road, Kuching.
Car hire
Petra Jaya Car Rental Travel & Tours, H1 Taman Sri Sarawak, Kuching, tel (082) 416755/416790;
Saga Servis, Bang Chew Fook Onn, Miri, tel (085) 413622.

Kuching
Luxury
Holiday Inn, Jl Tunku Abdul Rahman, P O Box 2362, tel (082) 423111, fax (082) 426169;
Hilton, Jl Tunku Abdul Rahman, P O Box 2396, tel (082) 248200, fax (082) 428984;
Riverside Majestic, Jl Tunku Abdul Rahman, P O Box 2928, tel (082) 247777, fax (082) 425858.
Holiday Inn Damai Beach, Santubong, P O Box 2870, tel (082) 411777, fax (082) 428911.
Batang Ai: Book via Hilton Reservation Service, Kuching Hilton or local travel agent.
Mid-range
Borneo Hotel, 30 C-H, Jl Tabuan, tel (082) 244122, fax (082) 254848;
Telang Usan Hotel, Jl Ban Hock, P O Box 1579, tel (082) 415588, fax (082) 425316.
Budget
Fata Hotel, 5-6 Jl McDougall, tel (082) 248111, fax (082) 428987;
Longhouse Hotel, 101 Jl Abell, tel (082) 419333, fax (082) 421563;
Orchid Inn, 2 Green Hill Road, tel (082) 411417, fax (082) 241635
Camp Permai:
Accommodation in log cabins, tree houses or tents: available to independent travellers. Book through Menara SEDC in Kuching on tel (082) 416777, fax (082) 244585.

Miri
Luxury
Righa Royal Hotel, Jl Temenggong Datuk Oyong, Lawai, P O Box 1145.
Mid-range
Gloria Hotel, 27 Brooke Road, P O Box 1283, tel (085) 416699, fax (085) 418866;
Harbour View Inn, Lot 124, Jl Bendahara, P O Box 1078, tel (085) 412177, fax (085) 420871.
Budget
Brooke Inn, 12 Brooke Road, P O Box 96, tel (085) 412881, fax (085) 420899;
Gaya (Air Cond) Inn, 23 Jl China, tel (085) 410022fax (085) 410218;

Sibu
Mid-range
Li Hua Hotel, Long Bridge Commercial Centre, tel (084) 324000, fax (084) 326272.
Budget
Capital Hotel, 19 Wong Nai Siong Road, tel (084) 336444, fax (084) 311706.

Mulu
Luxury
Royal Mulu Resort, CDT 62, Sungai Melinau, Miri, tel (085) 421122, fax (085) 421088: built in the style of a longhouse with all modern facilities and air-conditioning.
Budget
Alo Dada Inn, National Park, tel (085) 37408, fax (085) 415887;
Benarat Inn, Lorong Pala, National Park, tel (085) 419337, fax (085) 414503.

Sarawak at a Glance

WHERE TO EAT

Kuching
Eating out in Kuching is very inexpensive in food centres, hawkers' stalls and coffee shops, which usually serve Chinese or Malay food.

Bangkok Thai Seafood Restaurant, 317-319 Ground Floor, Bangunan Bee San, Jn Padungan, tel (082) 482181;

Hungry Horse, 202-204 Level 2, Bangunan Satok, Jl Satok, tel (082) 413395;

Koreana, the only Korean restaurant in town (opposite Hilton Hotel) serves very good authentic Korean food.

Lau Ya Keng, Jl Carpenter, specializes in Malaysian breakfast of rice porridge, noodles and other local delicacies.

Lok Thian Restaurant, 318-319, GF Bangunan Bee San, Jl Padungan, tel (082) 331310;

Thompson's Corner, Jalan Nanas, and **Permata Food Centre** near the Hilton Hotel: good value-for-money local dishes;

Toh Yuen, Chinese restaurant at the Hilton, and Mei San at the Holiday Inn both serve excellent Chinese cuisine.

Miri
Apollo Seafood Centre, 4G Jl Yu Seng Selatan, tel (085) 420813.

Sibu
Bee Jing Restaurant, 155 Kampung Nyabor, tel (084) 330391.

Damai
Buntal Seafood Village: a cluster of restaurants built on stilts over the sea, 25km (15 miles) north of Kuching. Most popular is **Lim Hock Ann**, famous for stir-fried giant prawns and crab dishes.

TOURS AND EXCURSIONS

Semengoh: Visit the sanctuary either through a tour operator who will obtain a permit for you, or go independently by bus. Take STC bus No. 6 from Kuching bus station to Penrissen and get off at the Forest Department Nursery at Semengoh. A 30 min trek on wooden walkway will lead you to the sanctuary.

Mulu: Flights via Malaysia Airlines Rural Air Service. There are also boat services but it is a long and tedious journey of about 8 hr and involves two changes of boats which can be unreliable at times of low water. Local tour operators will arrange accommodation, food, guide, transport and permit.

Local Tour Companies
Borneo Adventure, 55 Main Bazaar, Kuching, tel (082) 245666/245175, fax (082) 422626;

CPH Travel Agencies, 70 Jl Padungan, 93100 Kuching, tel (082) 243708/414921, fax (082) 424687;

Borneo Transverse Tours & Travel, 10-B 1st Floor, Wayang Street, 93000 Kuching, tel (082) 257784/257882, fax (082) 421419;

Agas-Pan Asia Travel, 2nd Floor, Unit R 206, Sarawak Plaza, Kuching, tel (082) 429754/428969, fax (082) 419754;

Tropical Adventure, Lot 228, 1st Floor, Jl Maju, Beautiful Jade Centre, P O Box 1433, 98000 Miri, tel (085) 451 9337, fax (085) 414503;

Transworld Travel Services, 2.04, 2nd Floor, Wisma Pelita Tunku, P O Box 42, 98007 Miri, tel (085) 356888, fax (085) 415277;

Sazhong Trading & Travel Service, No 4 Jl Central, 96000 Sibu, tel (084) 336017, fax (084) 338031.

USEFUL CONTACTS

Sarawak Tourist Information Centre at Main Bazaar or the **Malaysia Tourism Promotion Board** at Tingkat 2, Banggunan AIA, Bukit Mata Kuching, Jalan Song Thian Cheok, Kuching, tel (082) 246575/246775. There is also a Sarawak Tourist Association desk at Kuching airport.

KUCHING	J	F	M	A	M	J	J	A	S	O	N	D
AVERAGE TEMP. °F	78	78	80	80	82	82	82	82	80	80	80	80
AVERAGE TEMP. °C	26	26	27	27	28	28	28	28	27	27	27	27
Hours of Sun Daily	4	4	4	5	6	6	6	6	5	5	5	4
RAINFALL in	27	20	13	11	10	8	8	8	10	13	14	18
RAINFALL mm	683	522	330	286	253	199	199	211	271	326	343	465
Days of Rainfall	18	17	16	22	23	16	20	17	28	30	24	27

8
Sabah

Sabah, 'the Land below the Wind', lies in the north-eastern part of the island of Borneo. It has a coastline of 1440km (712 miles) with fine beaches on the west coast, mainly mangrove swamps on the east coast, and 38 reef islands. Like Sarawak, it has a strong ethnic background with some 32 indigenous communities, each with its own cultural heritage. The Chinese form the second largest population group, followed by the Indians and migratory groups from the Philippines and Indonesia.

Up to the 15th century, Sabah consisted of autonomous communities and various clans ruled by chieftains, all owing allegiance to the sultan of Brunei. Later, areas east of Marudu Bay were ceded to the sultan of Sulu in return for his help in settling a succession dispute. In 1881, an English businessman called Alfred Dent obtained a lease on the land from the sultans of Brunei and Sulu and established the Chartered Company of **British North Borneo**. Like most of Southeast Asia, it was occupied by the Japanese during World War II. At the end of the Japanese occupation in 1945, the Chartered Company gave up its rights to the British Government and Sabah became a British Crown Colony. In 1963, together with Sarawak, it became part of Malaysia.

Sabah is one of the most popular tourist destinations in Malaysia. Holidays in Sabah spell 'activity', from mountain climbing and cave exploration to diving in one of the richest marine havens in the world, while the richness of its cultural heritage will make your stay an enthralling experience.

CLIMATE

The weather pattern in Sabah is dictated by the mountains. In the north of the state the dry season runs from Dec–May, with the heaviest rainfall in Oct. In the south the rain is heaviest in Jan and lightest between Mar–Sep (though it still rains regularly). If you are planning to climb Mount Kinabalu, Feb–Apr is the driest time.

Opposite: *Ferns and mosses festoon the track through the montane forest at about 2150m (7000ft) on Mount Kinabalu.*

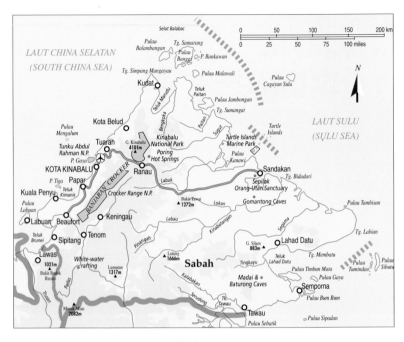

Kota Kinabalu ★

Known locally as KK, the capital city is a busy port and the international gateway to Sabah. There are no grand colonial buildings here, as most of the town, then known as Jesselton, was destroyed during the last days of the war. Half a day is sufficient to cover the main places of interest like the **State Mosque**, a majestic structure adorned with domes decorated with gold inlay motifs. It is located at Jalan Sembulan. The **State Museum** at Jalan Muzium gives a picture of Sabah, with its extensive collection of ethnological, archaeological and natural history exhibits. Opening hours are 10:00 to 18:00 from Monday to Thursday and 09:00 to 18:00 on Saturday and Sunday. It is closed on Friday. A trip up to the exclusive area of Signal Hill, with its fine houses and the **Istana**, gives a panoramic view of the town. You may also like to stroll through the **Central Market** and the market stalls at the seafront. Here you will find an array of local food,

DON'T MISS

★★★ Kinabalu National Park: Unrivalled variety of plants, including the world's largest flower.
★★★ Mount Kinabalu: Experience a tropical dawn at the summit of Southeast Asia's highest mountain.
★★★ Pulau Sipadan: A coral treasure trove.
★★★ Sepilok: A sanctuary for the threatened orang-utan.
★★ White-water rafting down the cascading waters of Sabah's beautiful rivers.

A peaceful scene by the waterfront in Kota Kinabalu, with Mount Kinabalu towering in the background.

traditional artefacts and forest produce amongst the vivid hustle and bustle.

Kinabalu National Park ★★★

A scenic two-hour drive from Kota Kinabalu takes you to this nature reserve which covers an area of 754km² (291sq miles). Its flora and fauna varies according to its altitude, from lowland forest up to 1300m (4270ft) to alpine vegetation in the summit zone above 3300m (13,000ft). At the Park Headquarters, 1524m (5000ft) above sea level, there are several miles of easy, graded trails leading to scenic viewpoints and clear mountain streams. The cool temperature is conducive to exploring the nature trails. Visitors can admire the diversity of plant life including wild orchids. This is the home of the largest flower in the world, the parasitic *Rafflesia*, which can measure 45cm (18ins) in diameter, though it can only be seen in selected areas of the park. There are daily guided tours of some of the trails (check in the Park Headquarters for times). About 43km (27 miles) from the Park Headquarters is **Poring Hot Springs** which has open-air sulphur baths immersed in a beautiful landscaped garden. Accommodation is available in chalets and hostels for those who want to savour the mountain air for longer than a day trip.

THE RICHES OF THE FOREST

Chinese trade with the peoples of Borneo is of very long standing, and as well as gold and diamonds, the island's exports have included some more unusual items:

● **Camphor:** best quality Bornean camphor was used in Chinese medicine to stimulate the heart and in embalming preparations.

● **Gaharu:** the local name for aloeswood or eagle's wood, a rare and costly fragrant resin.

● **Damar:** another resin, sometimes burned as a light source.

● **Bezoar stones:** found in the gall bladders of leaf monkeys, and used in various medicines and as an aphrodisiac.

● **Illipe nuts:** Borneans use illipe oil for cooking; in Europe it was made into candles and is now an ingredient in good quality lipsticks.

Mount Kinabalu ★★★

The highlight of the park is the climb to the summit of Mount Kinabalu, whose awesome granite massif dominates the terrain. No mountaineering skill is necessary but you must be physically fit to attempt the strenuous hike to the peak. To enjoy the scenery *en route* and to ease the journey to the top, a three days/two nights trip is recommended.

To reach the start of the summit trail, you can drive or walk from the Park Headquarters on the Kamborongoh Road for 4km (2.5 miles) to the Power Station at 1829m (6000ft). The trail follows a narrow ridge and dips into the main slope of Mount Kinabalu itself. A little further away is **Carson's Falls**, after which the trail begins to climb steeply to the first summit trail shelter at 1951m (6400ft). The second shelter is found at 2134m (7000ft) where the path climbs a steep narrow ridge before dipping into a mossy forest. Low's pitcher plants are found here, named after Hugh Low, who in 1851 was the first man to record his ascent of the mountain (though he failed to reach the summit).

The trail continues, offering shelters at various elevations. At 3353m (11,000ft), at **Panar Laban**, is the Laban

The craggy granite peaks of Mount Kinabalu seen from Panar Laban, where most climbers stay overnight before climbing to the summit to watch the dawn.

Rata rest-house. Here the first explorers stopped to sacrifice a white cockerel and seven eggs to appease the mountain spirits. Today, the ritual is carried out once a year. Most people stay here overnight before the final climb to the summit in the early hours of the morning. From Panar Laban the path climbs up a gully to the last shelters at **Sayat-Sayat**, where the white mountain-necklace orchids grow among the rocks. Here begins the vast expanse of grey granite which forms the summit plateau. **Low's Peak**, the summit itself, is not yet visible at this point. Most ascents are planned in time to see the sunrise. On a good clear day, almost all of Sabah is visible before the clouds shroud the mountain, usually at 09:00 or 10:00. From here you can see the awesome **Low's Gully**, a 1.25km (1 mile) deep chasm.

Climbers should respect the mountain and be prepared for its unpredictable weather. Make sure you bring some warm and waterproof clothing, packed in plastic bags to keep it dry. Trainers are adequate for climbing. Gloves, hats, water bottle, torchlight, some headache tablets and high energy snacks are essential. All climbers to the summit must be accompanied by registered guides. Familiarize yourself with the naturalist programmes at Park Headquarters before you set out.

Tunku Abdul Rahman Park ★★★
Only 20 minutes by boat from Kota Kinabalu is a cluster of five islands, gazetted as a State Park in 1974. **Pulau Sulug** is the furthest away from the city and has a small beach on its eastern side. It has good reef patches at the southern end of the island. There is no accommodation on the island but changing-rooms, toilets and picnic shelters are provided. **Pulau Mamutik**, the smallest of the group, is the nearest to Kota Kinabalu and hence very popular. It has excellent beaches with rich coral life surrounding the whole island, and a rest-house for overnight stays. A nature trail leading to the top of the island gives a good view of the reefs. **Pulau Manukan** has stretches of good beach especially at its eastern tip. The beautiful coral reef makes it an excellent spot for

An outstanding variety of plants grow on Mount Kinabalu.

Above: *A* Dendrochilum *species, one of an estimated 1200 species of orchid to be found there.*

Top: Rhododendron fallacinum, *growing at about 2700m (9000ft).*

THE BAJAU OF KOTA BELUD

The Bajau came from the Philippines in the 18th and 19th centuries, and one group settled around Kota Belud where they became farmers, raising buffaloes which they can still be seen buying and selling at the Kota Belud *tamu* each Sunday. They are skilled horsemen, often nicknamed the 'cowboys of the east'. On ceremonial occasions they ride bareback in elaborate jewelled costumes, carrying spears.

snorkelling and scuba diving. The Park Headquarters is located here, and there are chalets, a swimming pool, restaurants and a diving centre. **Pulau Sapi** is connected by a sand bar to Pulau Gaya. This island has one of the best beaches in the Park, and an excellent coral reef. There is no accommodation but picnic tables, shelters, changing-rooms and toilets are available. Camping is allowed with permission from the Park Warden or Sabah Parks Office in Kota Kinabalu. **Pulau Gaya**, the largest of the islands, is rich in flora and fauna, including sea eagles, hornbills, macaques, pangolin, wild pigs and reptiles. It has 16 miles of shoreline on which the most popular beach is at Bulijong Bay, known as Police Beach. There is no accommodation but the usual day facilities are available. There are regular boat and ferry services to the islands.

Tuaran *

This small town, about 35km (22 miles) from Kota Kinabalu, has lovely beaches fringed with casuarina trees. Every Sunday morning, the local people flock to its weekly market, or *tamu*. Traders and buyers come from far and wide to exchange goods ranging from livestock to traditional medicine, jungle produce, cakes, handicrafts, dried fish and spices, which are displayed on the ground or on small stalls.

Against this timeless setting is Sabah's first luxurious divers' centre, the **Sabandar Bay Resort**, sprawled along a beautiful beach. Newly opened in May 1994, it offers fully fledged facilities for scuba diving, with chalet-style accommodation shaded by casuarina trees, and the imposing profile of Mount Kinabalu clearly visible in the distance.

Bajau women come to sell their wares and catch up with the week's news at the large tamu *held every Sunday in Kota Belud, in the foothills of Mount Kinabalu.*

Pulau Sipadan ★★★

When the naturalist and diver, Jacques Cousteau, visited Sipadan in 1988, he remarked, 'I have seen other places like Sipadan – 45 years ago – but now no more. Now we have found again an untouched piece of art.' Sipadan is undoubtedly one of the best dive sites in the world. About three hours by boat from Semporna, on the southeast tip of Sabah, Sipadan is an underwater heaven. It is Malaysia's only oceanic island, mushrooming 600m (1970ft) from the bed of the Celebes Sea. It is a treasure trove of the underwater world with its wide variety of marine life: soft corals, sharks, turtles, fish of every size and colour, lobsters and barracudas. The shallow water around the island provides an ideal snorkelling ground while the excellent white coral sand and forested central core of the island offer non-divers opportunities for beachcombing and nature study. It is also a bird sanctuary with frigates, sea eagles and terns.

A palm-fringed island surrounded by clear shallow sea off the east coast of Sabah near Semporna.

Sandakan ★★

The old capital of British North Borneo, Sandakan was repeatedly bombed by the Allied Forces after the Japanese invasion in 1941. In 1945 the Japanese burned it to the ground and the capital moved to Jesselton. Today Sandakan is a bustling fishing port and its restaurants can claim to serve the best seafood in Malaysia. The interesting daily **fish market** is the biggest in Sabah. The **Japanese Cemetery** and the **Australian Memorial** are grim reminders of the Japanese occupation. The memorial marks the site of the prison camp from which the infamous Death March of 1945 began: 1800 Australian and 600 British prisoners of war forced to walk 227km (141 miles) through the jungle to Ranau. Only six survived to reach Ranau a year later.

Since its foundation in 1964, Sepilok Rehabilitation Centre is said to have released over 200 orang-utans back into the wild. This young inhabitant is about two years old.

Sepilok Orang-utan Rehabilitation Centre ★★★

At Sepilok, 24km (15 miles) from Sandakan, is a sanctuary for orang-utans rescued from captivity as well as those saved from forests cleared for agriculture. Orangutans are a protected species and it is illegal to keep them as pets in Malaysia. The main aim of the centre is to ease its inmates back to the wild through a process of learning and regaining their basic instinct to survive in the forest.

The twice daily feeding sessions, on platforms built in the trees, are a delight to watch. The orang-utans swing in from all directions to feed and frolic with one another or interact with the wildlife rangers. Unless you do not mind playing a game of tug-of-war with the apes, it is advisable not to wear anything bright or shiny which will attract their attention. Beware of nimble fingers if you are carrying a camera or handbag. Whilst they may look cuddly and tame, it is important to remember that these primates are wild animals. No attempt should be made to touch them or hold them. This is to prevent the spread of disease and to discourage their attachment to human beings. Sepilok is open daily from 09:00 to 12:00 and 14:00 to 16:00, except Fridays when it is closed between 11:30 and 14:00.

Kinabatangan and Gomantong Caves ★★

Nature enthusiasts will enjoy a trip on the **Kinabatangan River Safari**. Here in the swamps of the Lower Kinabatangan, you can see the strange-looking proboscis monkeys with their big protruding noses. The species is known as *Orang Belanda* or 'Dutchman', named after early Dutch missionaries whose European noses seemed large to the local people. These placid monkeys can be seen foraging for food by the riverside or crashing from tree to tree by the water. Orang-utans and elephants also inhabit this area but are rarely to be seen. Between the road to the village of Sukau and the Kinabatangan River lie the **Gomantong Caves**, home to millions of bats and swiftlets whose nests are much prized by the Chinese for birds' nest soup.

Proboscis monkeys inhabit the riverine forest along the banks of the Kinabatangan River. Only the males are endowed with huge pendulous noses: the females and young have small snub ones.

Turtle Islands Park ★★★

Lying some 40km (25 miles) off the coast north of Sandakan, lies a group of three islands which have been designated as the **Turtle Islands Park** under Sabah Parks authority. From July to October, green and hawksbill turtles come ashore to lay their eggs. **Pulau Selingaan** has furnished chalets for visitors for overnight stays. At night when the turtles heave themselves ashore to lay eggs, the park rangers will alert you. Accommodation should be pre-booked with Sabah Parks or you can arrange the whole trip through a tour company. The other two islands do not have overnight facilities but can be visited on day trips.

Shooting Rapids

White-water rafting is a growing sport among visitors to Sabah. The most popular location is the **Padas River** near Tenom, for experienced rafters only, reached by rail from Beaufort. The **Kedamaian River** in Kota Belud offers fairly fast rafting during the rainy season, while the **Mulau River** in the Kiulu area is suitable for beginners. The **Papar River** near Papar town with its rustic setting is one of the best rivers for shooting the rapids, with roller-coaster waters. These white-water areas are amongst the most scenic spots in Sabah.

BIRDS' NEST SOUP

The Chinese have been eating birds' nest soup for over a thousand years, and claim that it is both an aphrodisiac and a remedy for asthma. The nest material is blended with salt and chicken stock to make the soup, to which it imparts a unique glutinous texture. White nests fetch the highest price as they are pure swiftlet saliva, whereas the darker nests have to be painstakingly cleaned, using tweezers to pick out bits of feather and dirt.

A TRAIN RIDE ALONG THE PADAS GORGE

The only railway in Borneo, linking the towns of Papar, Beaufort and Tenom, opened in 1905 and is all that was built of the ambitious 'Trans-Borneo Railway' planned by the directors of the North Borneo Chartered Company. The line between Beaufort and Tenom runs along the side of the picturesque Padas Gorge, and the trains travel so slowly on the steep gradient that there is plenty of time to admire the view.

Sabah at a Glance

The best time to visit is between Mar–Oct. If you are planning to climb **Mount Kinabalu**, Feb–Apr is the driest time. The **Sabah Fest** occurs in May, with dance performances, handicraft exhibitions, food fair and carnival. The Kadazan harvest festival of **Pesta Ka'amatan** is celebrated on 30 and 31 May.

Sabah is served by some international airlines with direct flights from Singapore, Hong Kong, Manila, Bandar Seri Begawan (Brunei), Seoul, Taipei, Tokyo and Los Angeles. It is also accessible worldwide through Kuala Lumpur with Malaysia Airlines and from Singapore with Singapore Airlines. There are flights to Kuching and Miri in Sarawak and all major towns are served by Malaysia Airlines.

Buses and taxis operate within and between towns, while ferries serve the islands in **Tunku Abdul Rahman Park**. There is a rail service between **Tenom** and **Beaufort** through the Padas Gorge; for reservations, contact the Stationmaster on tel (087) 211518.
Bus companies
Labuk Road Bus Co, Jl Pryer, Sandakan, tel (089) 213142;
Leila Road Bus Co, Jl Pryer, Sandakan, tel (089) 212070. There are minibuses serving

other towns from Kota Kinabalu, departing from various points in the town centre.
Car Hire
Ais Rent-A-Car, Block A, Lot, 1, Ground Floor, Sinsuran Complex, Kota Kinabalu, tel (088) 238954/223022;
Borneo Car Rental, 5 1/2 mile, Lot 24, Likas Industrial Centre, Jl Tuaran, Kota Kinabalu, tel (088) 429041;
Kinabalu Rent A Car, Lot 3.60 & 3.61, Kompleks Karamunsing, Kota Kinabalu, tel (088) 232602.

Kota Kinabalu
Luxury
Shangri-la's Tanjung Aru Resort, Locked Bag 174, tel (088) 225800, fax (088) 217155: about ten minutes from the city centre. This deluxe resort does not have a beach front but it has a beautifully landscaped garden, restaurants, swimming pool, and a marina with a wide range of watersports.
Hyatt Kinabalu Hotel, Jl Datuk Salleh Sulong, tel (088) 221234, fax (088) 225972.
Mid-range
Hotel Shangri-la, 75 Bandaran Berjaya, P O Box 11718, tel (088) 212800, fax (088) 212078 (not connected with the international chain of Shangri-la Hotels);
Palace Hotel, 1 Jl Tangki Karamunsing, P O Box 10453, tel (088) 211911, fax (088) 211600;
Capital Hotel, 23 Jl Haji

Saman, P O Box 11223, tel (088) 231999, fax (088) 237222;
Hotel Jesselton, 69 Jl Gaya, tel (088) 55633, fax (088) 240401.
Budget
Ang's Hotel, 28 Jl Bakau G, P O Box 10843, tel (088) 234999, fax (088) 217867;
City Inn, 41 Jl Pantai, P O Box 10025, tel (088) 218933, fax (088) 218937;
Golden Inn, Block M, Lot 5-6-7, Sinsuran Complex, tel (088) 211510, fax (088) 231198.
In addition, the **Sukan Sports Complex Hostel** offers inexpensive rooms.

Sandakan
Luxury
Sandakan Renaissance Hotel, Km 1, Jl Utara, P O Box 275, tel (089) 213299, fax (089 271271: the only international hotel in Sandakan.
Mid-range
Sanbay Hotel, P O Box 211, tel (089) 275000, fax (089) 275575;
City View Hotel, Lot 1, Block 23, 3rd Avenue, P O Box 624, tel (089) 271122, fax (089) 273115.
Budget
May Fair Hotel, 24 Jl Pryer, P O Box 512, tel (089) 219812.

Tuaran
Sabandar Dive Resort, off Jl Pantai Dalit, Jl Sabandar, tel (088) 242884, fax (088) 249946 (HQ in Kota Kinabalu).

Sabah at a Glance

WHERE TO EAT

Foodwise, as in every part of Malaysia, hawkers stalls and coffee shops offer the best value for money meals while all the major hotels have their own outlets serving local as well as western cuisine.

Kota Kinabalu
Jaws Seafood Restaurant, Karamunsing Warehouse, tel (088) 236009;
Port View Seafood Restaurant, Jl Haji Saman;
100% Seafood Restaurant, Tanjung Aru Beach;
Windbell Seafood Restaurant, Jl Selangor, Tanjung Aru, tel (088) 222305;
Restaurant Sri Melaka, 9 Jl Laiman, Diki, tel (088) 224777: Nonya cooking.

Sandakan
Penang Food Centre, 4 Bandar Ramai-Ramai, tel (089) 45335;
Canny Seafood Restaurant, Bandar Leila, tel (089) 43602;
Golden Palace Restaurant, Trigg Hill, tel (088) 211878: Chinese, seafood.

TOURS AND EXCURSIONS

Mount Kinabalu: Reservations for guide, porter and accommodation must be made at the Park's Head Office in Kota Kinabalu at the Sinsuran Complex. To get to the Park by public transport take the Ranau bus from the Padang at Kota Kinabalu or hire a taxi. Alternatively you can book the trip through a local tour operator.
Sabandar Bay: For reservations and further information, contact **Borneo Endeavou**r, 2nd Floor, Lot 10, Block A, Damai Plaza, Lorong Pokok Kayi Manis, Luyang, 883300 Kota Kinabalu, tel (088) 249950, fax (088) 249946.
Sipadan: For reservations and further information, contact **Borneo Divers and Sea Sports**, 4th Floor, Wisma Sabah, Jalan Haji Saman, Kota Kinabalu, tel (088) 222226, fax (088) 221550, or **Sipadan Dive Centre** at 1004 Wisma Merdeka, Jalan Tun Razak, 88000 Kota Kinabalu, Sabah, tel (088) 240584, fax (088) 240415.
Sepilok: A visit to Sepilok involves a very early start at about 06:00 if you are flying in from Kota Kinabalu. You can reach it by taxi from Sandakan airport (make sure you arrange with the taxi-driver for your return trip) or by bus. Look out for buses labelled 'Sepilok Batu 14' from the Bus Station on the waterfront. Check the timetable with the Labuk Road Bus Company.
Kinabatangan and Gomantong: It is best to organize these trips through local tour companies who will arrange for transport and guides.

Local Tour Companies
Api Tours, Ground Floor, Wisma Sabah Jl Haji Saman, P O Box 12853, 88831 Kota Kinabalu, tel (088) 221233, fax (088) 221230: for white-water rafting trips;
Borneo Eco Tours, 3rd Floor, Lot 6, Block J, Sadong Jaya, 88100 Kota Kinabalu, tel (088) 234009, fax (088) 233688;
Exotic Borneo Holidays, Suite B, 1st Floor, Lot 24, Likas Industrial Centre, Tuaran Road, 8856 Kota Kinabalu, tel (088) 429224/429041, fax (088) 429024.

USEFUL CONTACTS

Sabah Tourism Promotion Corporation at 51 Jalan Gaya, 88000 Kota Kinabalu, Sabah, Malaysia, tel (088) 218620/212121, fax (088) 212075. Postal Address: Mail Bag 112, 88999 Kota Kinabalu, Sabah.
Malaysia Tourism Promotion Board, Ground Floor, Wisma Wing Onn Life, 1 Sagunting, Kota Kinabalu, tel (088) 248698/211732, fax (088) 241764.

KOTA KINABALU	J	F	M	A	M	J	J	A	S	O	N	D
AVERAGE TEMP. °F	78	77	80	80	82	80	80	78	80	80	80	78
AVERAGE TEMP. °C	26	25	27	27	28	27	27	26	27	27	27	26
Hours of Sun Daily	6	7	8	8	8	7	7	7	6	6	6	6
RAINFALL in	5	3	2	4	9	11	9	10	11	13	12	9
RAINFALL mm	129	64	61	112	226	291	255	260	285	336	297	230
Days of Rainfall	10	7	6	8	13	13	13	13	15	16	16	13

Travel Tips

Tourist Information

The Malaysian Tourism Promotion Board (Tourism Malaysia) has overseas offices in Australia, Canada, France, Germany, Hong Kong, Korea, Japan, Netherlands, Singapore, Taiwan, Thailand, United Kingdom and USA.
Headquarters: 17, 24th-27th Floor, Menara Dato' Onn, Putra World Trade Centre, 45 Jl Tun Dr Ismail, 50480 Kuala Lumpur, tel (03) 293 5188, fax (03) 293 5884;
The board's regional offices are located in Penang, Johor Bahru, Kuala Terengganu, Kuching and Kota Kinabalu: consult the relevant chapters for addresses/telephone numbers, and for details of local tourist information centres.

Entry Documents

All visitors to Malaysia must be in possession of a valid national passport or other travel document recognized by the Malaysian Government. Such a passport or travel document must have at least 6 months validity beyond the period of stay permitted in Malaysia.

Visas: 1. The following do not need visas to enter Malaysia as bona fide visitors: Commonwealth citizens (except India, Bangladesh, Pakistan and Sri Lanka), British protected persons whose returnability to the country of origin is assured, and citizens of Switzerland, Netherlands, San Marino and Liechtenstein. 2. Citizens of the following countries do not need visas for stays not exceeding the duration of three months if they hold full national passports (for a longer stay or purpose of employment, a visa is required): Albania, Algeria, Argentina, Austria, Bahrain, Belgium, Czech Republic, Denmark, Egypt, Finland, Germany, Hungary, Iceland, Italy, Japan, Jordan, Kuwait, Lebanon, Luxembourg, Morocco, Norway, Oman, Qatar, Saudi Arabia, Slovakia, South Korea, Sweden, Tunisia, Turkey, United Arab Emirates, USA and Yemen.
Visa Relaxation: 1. No visa is required for nationals of members of the Association of South East Asian Nations (ASEAN), i.e. Indonesia,

Philippines, Thailand, Singapore and Brunei, for a visit up to one month.
2. Nationals of Bulgaria, Rumania and CIS do not require a visa for a stay of up to one week.
3. Nationals of Afghanistan, Iran, Iraq, Libya and Syria do not require a visa for a visit of up to two weeks.
4. Citizens of other countries not mentioned above do not require a visa for a stay of up to one month.
Note: The concessions mentioned in (1) , (2) and (3) are for the purposes of tourism and business only. Visitors must have entry facilities to a destination beyond Malaysia and must be in possession of a confirmed air ticket. For any further stay or purpose of employment, a visa is required.

A visa is required by holders of Certificate of Identity, Titre De Voyage, or holders of a national passport of India, Nepal, Bhutan, Sri Lanka, Pakistan, Bangladesh, Taiwan, People's Republic of China, Cuba, Mongolia, Myanmar, North Korea and Vietnam.

The application has to be referred to Immigration Headquarters in Kuala Lumpur (see below) for approval. Please note that all such applications must have a Malaysian sponsor.

Director General of Immigration Malaysia, Immigration Headquarters, Block I, Level 1-7, Jalan Damansutra, Pusat Bandar Damansara, Damansara Height, 50550 Kuala Lumpur, Malaysia, tel (03) 255 5077, fax (03) 256 2340.

• Nationals of Israel, Serbia and Montenegro are not allowed to enter the country.

TRAFFICKING IN ILLEGAL DRUGS CARRIES THE DEATH PENALTY

Health Requirements

Smallpox and yellow fever vaccinations are not required for travellers entering Malaysia, except for those who have visited endemic zones 14 days (for smallpox) or 6 days (for yellow fever) prior to arriving in the country. Children under one year old (for yellow fever) and six months (for smallpox) are exempted.

Getting to Malaysia

Malaysia is accessible by sea, road and, most conveniently, by air. The national airline, Malaysia Airlines, flies from most major cities in the world. Malaysia is also served by 22 other airlines. Check with your travel agent. There are international airports at Kuala Lumpur, Penang, Kuantan, Langkawi, Kota Kinabalu and Kuching. Arriving by sea, the ports are Penang, Port Klang, Kuantan, Kuching and Kota Kinabalu. There is a highway link from Singapore to Thailand through Malaysia.

Airport tax is collected at the airport upon departure at airline check-in desks. For domestic flights the tax is RM5.00. For international flights, it is RM20.00. The exact change is required.

Getting Around Malaysia

Air: Malaysia Airlines operates a comprehensive network of domestic routes to and from the following destinations: Alor Setar, Bintulu, Ipoh, Johor Bharu, Kota Bahru, Kota Kinabalu, Kuala Lumpur, Kuala Terengganu, Kuantan, Kuching, Lahad Datu, Langkawi, Miri, Penang, Sandakan, Sibu and Tawau. Head office: Bangunan MAS, Jl Sultan Ismail, 50250 Kuala Lumpur.
Pelangi Air runs services from Kuala Lumpur, Ipoh and Penang to some smaller towns and resorts: Sitiawan, Alor Setar, Langkawi, Melaka, Taman Negara, Pulau Tioman, Kuantan, Kerteh and Kuala Terengganu.

Rail: Malaysian Railways, or Keretapi Tanah Melayu (KTM) offers a comfortable and economical means of travelling round the Peninsula. One main line runs up the west coast, north from Singapore through Kuala Lumpur and Butterworth to meet Thai Railways at the border; the other branches off at Gemas and goes north to Kota Bharu on the east coast, also linking with Thai Railways. There are express or regular services: the latter are slightly cheaper but with more stops. There is only one railway line in East Malaysia, from Kota Kinabalu to Tenom in Sabah.

Roads: Malaysia has a good road network: the North-South Expressway runs up the west coast of the Peninsula from Singapore to the Thai border, the East West Highway connects Butterworth and Kota Bharu in the north, and further south a third highway crosses the country from Kuala Lumpur to Karak and Kuantan (tolls are charged on some stretches). Towns in Sabah and Sarawak are connected by roads along the coast. Hire cars are readily available to holders of an International Driving Licence. Driving is on the left in Malaysia, and the speed limit in towns is 50kmph. The wearing of seatbelts is compulsory in front seats.

ROAD SIGNS

Most road signs are international, but the following local signs should be noted:
Awas Caution
Ikut kiri Keep left
Kurangkan laju Slow down
Jalan sehala One way
Utara North
Selatan South
Timur East
Barat West
Berhenti Stop

Taxis: As well as local taxis, long-distance taxis travel between states connecting all major towns, operating on a shared-cost basis once the driver has filled his vehicle with travellers going to the same destination. Most local taxis now have meters; if yours does not, negotiate the fare in advance.

Buses: Air-conditioned express buses connect the major towns; there are also non-air-conditioned buses (with lower fares) running between and within the states.

Trishaws: These are still available in Melaka, Georgetown, Kota Bharu and many smaller towns and are an excellent way to get around.

Boats: Express boats ply the larger rivers in Sarawak, otherwise a local boat may usually be chartered at a price. Towards the end of the dry season in East Malaysia some rivers may become unnavigable in part, and may swell dangerously during the monsoon. Regular ferry services connect the principal islands with the mainland. Smaller islands can be reached in local boats from the nearest port.

Accommodation

Malaysia has accommodation to suit all budgets in most locations, from international class hotels to more modest hotels and rest houses, as well as 'homestay' accommodation with families in East Coast kampungs, 'A'-frame huts on beaches and campsites. All room rates are subject to a 5% government tax and 10% service charge. A selection of recommendations is given for each region.

Eating out

To the Malaysians, food is a very serious business and the nation has transformed eating into an art form. Some even declare that they 'live to eat'. This is by no means to say they are a nation of gluttons but rather that they appreciate carefully prepared food and place an emphasis on quality rather than quantity. Their love of eating out is reflected in the number of food outlets available in every nook and corner of every town. A man with a wok and a stove is licensed to start a hawker's stall anywhere and coffee-shops double up as cheap restaurants. You can eat as cheaply or as expensively as you like.

Money Matters

Currency: The unit of currency is the Malaysian Ringgit (RM) which is divided into 100 *sen* (cents). Currency notes are issued in denominations of RM1, RM5, RM10, RM20, RM50, RM100, RM500, RM1,000. Coins are issued in 1, 5, 10, 20 and 50*sen* and RM1.

Banks: There are more than 40 commercial banks in Malaysia, with 580 branches throughout the country. Banking hours are: Monday to Friday 10:00–15:00, Saturday 9:30–11:30. In Kedah, Perlis, Kelantan and Terengganu, banks are open from 9:30–11:30 on Thursday and are closed on Friday.

Credit cards and travellers' cheques: Major credit cards and travellers cheques are widely accepted in most big establishments, departmental stores and hotels. For more favourable rates, travellers cheques are best exchanged at banks.

Tipping: A service charge of 10% plus a government tax of 5% is automatically added to your bill at restaurants and hotels, so tipping is not necessary unless you feel the service has been exceptionally good. There is no need to tip taxi drivers or attendants at food stalls.

Business hours

Shops are normally open from 9:30–19:00 while supermarkets and departmental stores open from 10:00–22:00. In Johor, Kedah, Perlis, Kelantan and Terengganu, some shops are closed on Fridays instead of Sundays.

Government office hours: Monday to Thursday 8:00–12:45 and 14:00–16:15, Friday 8:00–12:15 and 14:45–16:15, Saturday 8:00–12:45. In Johor, Kedah, Perlis, Kelantan and Terengganu, offices open for a half day on Thursday from 8:00–12:45 and are closed all day on Friday.

Public Holidays

As a result of its diversity of ethnic groups and religions, Malaysia has a large number of holidays during the year. In addition to the main religious celebrations, the sultans' birthdays are also holidays in the relevant states, and there are other national holidays. Islamic and Chinese festival dates are based on the lunar calendar and thus vary each year. Many businesses and all government offices close on public holidays; most shops and restaurants remain open except during Ramadan. The Malaysian Tourism Promotion Board publishes a list of holiday dates each year.

Telephones

Public telephone booths are available in supermarkets, departmental stores and post offices. You will need 10 sen coins for local calls. Long distance calls are best made from your hotel. Telephone cards are also available and come in denominations of RM3.00 to RM50.00. There are two types of card phones: 'Kadfon' which can only be used at Telekom phone booths, and 'Unicard' which can only be used at Uniphone booths. Telephone cards can be purchased at airports, petrol stations (Shell and Petronas) and most outlets of *7-Eleven* and *Hop-In*. For Directory Enquiries, dial 103.

Electricity

Mains voltage in Malaysia is 220 volts and uses three-pin plugs.

Weights and Measures

Malaysia uses metric measurements in all cases, although some milestones are marked in both kilometres and miles.

CONVERSION CHART		
FROM	TO	MULTIPLY BY
millimetres	inches	0.0394
metres	yards	1.0936
metres	feet	3.281
kilometres	miles	0.6214
hectares	acres	2.471
litres	pints	1.760
kilograms	pounds	2.205
tonnes	tons	0.984

To convert °Celsius to °Fahrenheit: x 9 ÷ 5 + 32

Time

Malaysian Standard Time is eight hours ahead of Greenwich Mean (Universal Standard) Time, seven hours ahead of Central European Winter Time, and 13 hours ahead of the USA's Eastern Standard Winter Time.

Health Services

In most major cities, medical centres offer the best health service. Private clinics are available even in the small towns. There are government hospitals throughout the country but they are more geared to the needs of the local population. Pharmacies dispensing western as well as Chinese traditional medicine are found mainly in departmental stores and supermarkets. Most international hotels have chemists' shops on their premises.

Avoiding Problems

Heat: It takes time to get used to the tropical heat and humidity. Take tepid showers and drink large amounts of water; use salt on food. Wear a shady hat and use a high-

factor suntan lotion to avoid sunburn. Wear loose clothing made of natural fibres.

Stomach upsets: Take care not to eat uncooked fish or meat and seek local advice on the quality of shellfish; peel your own fruit. Water is clean and safe in major cities in the Peninsula, but in other areas tap and stream water may be contaminated, especially during the monsoon season, and should be boiled. Bottled water is widely available.

Insects: Keep mosquitoes away by sleeping off the ground, under a net. Use an insect repellent. Malaria tablets are recommended if you plan to visit the forested interior and rural areas.

Bites and stings: Avoid walking in long grass with bare feet or in sandals or shorts. If you are bitten by a snake or other venomous creature, try to catch it for identification. Check for spiders or scorpions inside your shoes before putting them on.

Emergencies

Dial 999 for police, ambulance or fire.

Language

Although Bahasa Malaysia is the official language, English is widely spoken and is still the language used in communication amongst the various races throughout Malaysia. The English spoken among the Malaysians is commonly known as 'Manglish' - Malaysian English - which is a combination of local dialects with the English language. Malay grammar is very simple, with no articles, tenses or genders; plurals are rendered by doubling the word. Making the effort to use a few basic words and phrases will make you very popular with the Malaysians.

Greetings

how are you?/I am fine *apa khabar?/khabar baik*
good morning *selamat pagi*
good afternoon *selamat petang*
good night *selamat malam*
goodbye *selamat tinggal*
bon voyage *selamat jalan*
all right/good *baik*
thank you/you're welcome *terima kasih/sama sama*

Pronouns

I/me *saya*
we/us *kami*
you *anda/awak*
he/him/she/her *dia*
they/them *mereka*

Useful questions

can you help me? *bolehkah tolong saya?*
how do I get there? *bagaimanakah saya boleh ke sana*
how far? *berapa jauh?*
how much? (price) *berapa harganya?*
what is this/that? *apakah ini/itu?*
when? *bila?*
where? *di mana?*
why? *mengapa?*

Food

cold *sejuk*
to drink *minum*
to eat *makan*
hot (heat) *panas*
hot (spicy) *pedas*
ice *ais*
beef *daging lembu*
bread *roti*
chicken *ayam*
coffee *kopi*
crab *ketam*
egg *telur*
fish *ikan*
fruit *buah*
mutton *daging kambing*
pork *daging babi*
prawn *udang*
salt *garam*
sugar *gula*
tea *teh*
water (or a drink) *air*

Geographical features

beach *pantai*
bay *teluk*
cape *tanjung*
island *pulau*
hill *bukit*
mountain *gunung*
river *sungai*
sea *laut*

Useful words

airport *lapangan terbang*
aeroplane *kapal terbang*
a little *sedikit*
a lot *banyak*
bus *bas*
boat *kapal*
do not have *tiada*

excuse me *maafkan saya*
female *perempuan*
good *bagus*
have *ada*
I am sorry *saya minta maaf*
male *lelaki*
money *wang/duit*
no *tidak* (more usually 'tak')
please *tolong/sila*
shop *kedai*
toilet *tandas/bilik air*
trishaw *beca*
train *keretapi*
railway station *stesyen kere tapi*
yes *ya*

Numbers

one *satu*
two *dua*
three *tiga*
four *empat*
five *lima*
six *enam*
seven *tujuh*
eight *lapan*
nine *sembilan*
ten *sepuluh*
eleven *sebelas*
twelve *dua belas*
twenty *dua puluh*
twenty-one *dua puluh satu*
one hundred *seratus*
two hundred *dua ratus*
one thousand *seribu*

Directions

go up *naik*
go down *turun*
turn *belok*
right *kanan*
left *kiri*
front *hadapan*
behind *belakang*
street *lebuh*
lane *lorong/pesiaran*
highway *lebuhraya*
toll *tol*
junction *simpang*

INDEX

Page numbers in *italics* refer to captions accompanying illustrations